# The
# *Lazy Girl's*
# *Party Guide*

Anita Naik is a freelance journalist who has written for *New Woman*, *Zest*, *Red*, *Cosmopolitan* and *Glamour*. Specialising in health and lifestyle issues, Anita was the agony aunt on *Just 17*. She is currently the agony aunt and health editor on *Closer* magazine.

Anita is also the author of:
*The Lazy Girl's Guide to a Fabulous Body*
*The Lazy Girl's Guide to Beauty*
*The Lazy Girl's Guide to Good Health*
*The Lazy Girl's Guide to Good Sex*

# The
# *Lazy Girl's Party Guide*

## Anita Naik

PIATKUS

## ✿ *Visit the Piatkus website!*

Piatkus publishes a wide range of bestselling fiction and non-fiction, including books on health, mind, body & spirit, sex, self-help, cookery, biography and the paranormal.

*If you want to:*
- read descriptions of our popular titles
- buy our books over the internet
- take advantage of our special offers
- enter our monthly competition
- learn more about your favourite Piatkus authors

VISIT OUR WEBSITE AT: www.piatkus.co.uk

First published in 2004 by
Piatkus Books Limited
5 Windmill Street
London W1T 2JA

e-mail: info@piatkus.co.uk

*A catalogue record for this book is available from the British Library*

ISBN 0 7499 2515 9

Text design by skeisch and Paul Saunders
Edited by Jan Cutler
Cover and inside illustrations by Nicola Cramp

This book has been printed on paper manufactured with respect for the environment using wood from managed sustainable resources

Printed and bound in Great Britain by Antony Rowe Ltd, Chippenham, Wiltshire

# contents

# acknowledgements

With thanks to the following: Helen Prangnell for party tips, Hayley Eaton for trying the black dress plan and Jenni and Tony P. who know how to party with the best (and probably have)!

Special thanks to personal trainer, Kieran Mullins, for the Little Black Dress Plan.

Kieran has over ten years of experience in physiology, bio-mechanics and nutrition. He also has a degree in physical education, and qualifications in YMCA personal training and from Holmes Place Academy of Personal Trainers. He's trained to coach football and boxing, and designed the bikini fit plan in *The Lazy Girl's Guide to a Fabulous Body*.

# introduction

'Parties are like meetings' a friend of mine once said, 'most of the time you can't be bothered to go, but how annoying is it if you don't get an invitation?' This from the girl who turned up embarrassingly late for her own thirtieth birthday party and later ruined her sister's engagement by accidentally falling on to the cake!

Another friend now refuses point-blank to step foot near a party for fear that she might look, do, say or act in an undignified manner (having scored 10/10 on all those counts over the last two years alone). If, like her, you're someone who has ever woken up post-party with a dark foreboding that you did something terrible but can't quite remember what – this is the survival guide for you.

Also, being a quintessential Lazy Girl's Guide it's also worth noting that this book is about throwing parties, because while it's not brain surgery to invite a few people over, the fact remains that most people don't like to do it for three main reasons: (1) the fear that people may not come; (2) the fear that people will come; and (3) the fear that you will be the host of the most boring party in the history of the world.

So, unless you're one of those annoying domestic-goddess types – adept at making your own invitations, knocking up a few fancy food bites, throwing together cocktails that rival the trendiest bar in town – then stick around for some killer hostess tips.

This guide is, after all, about how to party and survive it (and without looking as if you've been dragged through a hedge backwards). Read on to find out how to throw the best party of your life without being so fraught with fear that you drink yourself into oblivion before your guests arrive. Also discover how to pour yourself into a sexy dress with our fabulous four-week exercise plan, and learn how to be a guest in a million without being roped into doing all the hard work.

Finally, if you're looking for love, try out the perfect naughty-but-nice road map to party flirting! Most importantly of all, whatever your party aims, it pays to try out our magic hangover solutions. Try the lazy girl magic tips and you'll not only survive the morning after the night before but also be the winner of the party season.

# chapter 1

# How to be a party goddess

Like most people, you've been to some great parties in your time: maybe exotic ones in breathtaking locations or glamorous ones surrounded by gorgeous people where you had to take a week off to recover. Having said that, it's also likely that some of the best parties you've attended have been a spur-of-the-moment what's-this-cheap-plonk-we're-drinking kind of do! Not so glamorous, or so crowded, but at the end of the day just as enjoyable as the ones that came with fancy laminated invitations. And therein lies the joy of parties: you can't tell what one's going to be like from its cover! Meaning that party enjoyment comes not just from the fancy packaging but from what's on the inside too.

So, if you're currently thinking of throwing a party, this is the best fact to know and remember. However, if you want to guarantee your party goes with a bang rather than a whimper, you'll also have to do more than invite some friends over and blow up the odd balloon. Parties take effort and organisation – killer words for most lazy girls but the good news is: you can do it – and without having a nervous breakdown!

# *Throwing a party*

## *Step one: make a decision*

To be a party goddess, the most important thing is not deciding what you're going to wear and/or how to get that man you fancy to come and play (though if this is your aim let me direct you to Chapters 2 and 4). It's basically what kind of party you're going to have and who you are going to party with. This is because whether you like it or not, throwing a party is never a case of 'It's MY party and I'll do what I want to'; it's also about entertaining others.

Stray from that and you'll either end up partying alone or be known as the person who threw the worst party EVER. This means appropriateness is the name of the game. It's no good throwing a come-as-your-favourite-rock-slut party if the party is for your 68-year-old grand-mother. Likewise if you're trying to make a glamorous impression on your smart in-laws it's best not to suggest an engagement party with Disney characters. It's also wise to throw out the idea of a swanky cocktail party if most of your friends like to knock back kegs of beer while wearing their underpants. It's not that a party like this will be avoided at all costs, but more that you'll be the only one in a posh frock while everyone else drinks beer from your expensive Martini glasses.

## Step two: *think about your guests*

Trust me: never ever choose a theme that will make your guests feel awkward and/or unhappy before they even RSVP. This is important, as the whole idea of having a party is to have guests and impress your friends with your hostess skills. This is just one reason to knock that old party favourite – the fancy dress event – on its head.

Themes of the fancy dress nature, although good in print are, believe it or not, the kiss of death to people eagerly searching out a good time. If it seems like a fantastic idea to make everyone you love come as their favourite cartoon character, the chances are you're doing it only because: (a) you already have a good costume; (b) you want to humiliate your friends; and/or (c) you truly believe fancy dress will jazz up an otherwise boring event. The reality is fancy dress parties only ever work if the majority of your friends are out-of-work actors, if it's New Year's Eve, and/or if you promise copious amounts of alcohol to the best outfit (and even then that will entice only a third of your guests).

Fancy dress parties also put off the shy, the low self-esteemers, most men, and basically anyone with a shred of dignity. So repeat after me: if you are over the age of 12 years never ever have a costume party.

Having said that, party themes can work (see page 12) because they can give people a clear idea of the kind of party you're throwing. Birthdays, engagements, new house and New Year parties are all obvious to guests. Outdoor parties thrown in the summertime also are clear drinking/sun worshipping/BBQ fests. However, all other parties randomly thrown will make your guests fall into an 'Oh-my-god-what-are-you-wearing-is-it-her-birthday?' frenzy of anxiety. Meaning, if it is your birthday (and especially if you want gifts), say so.

Also, be clear about what kind of event you're throwing: is it a big party, a dinner party, a casual let's-call-in-a-pizza or something altogether more ornate. Your friends won't thank you if they turn up dressed like sexy divas only to find they'll be playing Twister all night or turn up in jeans to find everyone else in glam mode.

### Step three: be clear on your invitation

Whether your invitation is verbal, by email or by post – be consistent about what you're telling people (see page 18). Think date, times and special instructions, such as 'the front door is round the back of the house, and I live in London, England, not London, Canada'. For this reason avoid at all costs word-of-mouth invitations, because these will turn into a game of Chinese whispers, transforming your intimate brunch for six on Saturday into a weekender for 60 with food and booze supplied by yours truly.

To ensure this rule is applied at all times make sure you avoid the following cardinal sin of invitations: never invite people when you're drunk and never say the words 'BRING ANYONE YOU WANT', unless, of course, you want the local rugby and football clubs to turn up on your doorstep. If you've got to grips with all of that, here's how to plan the best party in the world.

*tip*

Think about every-one's needs. Always throw parties that take into account your guests' needs as well as your own.

# *What's this party for?*

This is the question you should always start with, especially if the last party you had was of the jelly, ice cream and pass-the-parcel variety. If you've never thrown a party in your life, the idea can either seem daunting and/or simple, both of which are incorrect. Fall into either camp and you'll have either a nervous breakdown on the night of your party or be known as the worst party thrower in the world.

The truth is, if the initial thought of having to clear-up post-party doesn't make you want to throw in the towel right away, then the idea of having to invite/plan/sit around and wait for people to turn up should have you

shaking in your boots. Why? Well, because when you say you're having a party, you are basically saying to friends, 'Come round for a good time at my expense'. While somewhat glib, that's basically what people hear when you say the magic word 'party'. Therefore, whether you like it or not, you have to put some thought into your event.

### Thought one: what are you celebrating (if anything)?

This will give you an instant idea about dates, venue and timings, as well as guest numbers and how much catering effort you have to put in.

### Thought two: where will the party be?

Tempting as it is to gloss over this one until the last minute, think carefully about the venue so you can estimate space and, therefore, numbers. Can your flat/house really hold 100 people without the floor caving in? Could you really find 50 people to fill that room above the pub? Be realistic.

### Thought three: what day shall I have it on?

A midweek dinner party can work if it's not a late do, Friday night events are better if they are at a venue and Saturday nights are best if you're doing it from your own place.

### Thought four: how many people should I invite?

Friends, lovers, friends of friends, work acquaintances, someone you once met at a bus stop ... how far are you willing to go and why?

### Thought five: what's the very least I have to do on the organisation front?

Though this is thought five, if you're very lazy it should probably be thought number one. Ironically, less isn't more when it comes to parties. A small dinner party may well take more effort from you than a drinks party for 20. Areas to think about include: invitations, adequate notice of the event, music, food and drink preparation, decor and cleaning up.

### Thought six: can I afford it?

Parties are more expensive than you think, especially if you're paying for a venue, a semi-free bar or even offering one in your own house. If you're working on the bring-a-bottle theme, you still need to offer more than a soft drink, a packet of roasted peanuts and a family-sized bag of crisps to your guests.

# Who are you inviting and why?

Friends, Romans, countrymen … people you've met at the bus stop? If all these people are on your list, then you need to be more discerning with your invitations. While it's tempting to invite the world and his brother, it's wiser to not get carried away with numbers. Apart from the obvious problem of space, it costs money to have more people. If it's in your house it's even more important to invite only people you know, like and trust. That is, trust to turn up, trust not to steal the silver and more importantly trust not to pass out on your bed at 3.00 a.m.

*tip*

Don't over-invite. Avoid inviting people when you're drunk, and avoid over-inviting just because you're afraid people won't turn up.

If, however, you are working on the more-the-merrier principle, it is worth inviting 10 per cent more people than you can comfortably fit into your venue. This is because no matter how eager people are when you invite them, when the day comes round at least 15 per cent of your guests won't turn up owing to sickness/health/memory problems and/or a wardrobe falling on top of them.

If you're seriously worried that you'll end up with a half-empty party, then tell ten of your most reliable friends to bring two people each. Thus, ensuring a guaranteed full party and a happy mix of people.

# The guest list

If making up a guest list is proving to be horribly stressful, then the chances are you're worrying too much about who is going to get on with whom. While it is your job to put all the preparation in place for an enjoyable party, it's not your job to ensure that each and every guest laughs all the time and doesn't come face to face with the ex who once dumped them by text message. Repeat after me: it's not your responsibility to ensure everyone is fabulously happy at your party. Guests, by the nature of being invited, are agreeing to come along and make your party good – meaning they are agreeing to have a good time all on their own.

As for the guest list, if you're stuck, start by imagining you are throwing a Hollywood red-carpet affair, where only ten people can come. These ten should be pretty easy to rattle off the top of your head, and are what's known as your core guests: people who will come even if hurricane-force winds are blowing outside.

Next, list the party people: the friends who are known for being great party animals and are excellent at whipping everyone into a frenzy of dancing/drinking/flirting. Then list groups of people: friends from college/school, friends from work, friends you see on your own and friends of friends you've always wanted to meet. Finally, make a reserve list, although obviously this is a secret list never to be revealed to anyone: these are the people who get invited when someone drops off your initial list, and are your fillers. It's tough but that's parties for you, if everyone was invited you'd need to hire a stadium.

# What kind of party are you throwing?

OK, this is the theme section. Having already hopefully put you off fancy dress parties, this is the place where you can be creative about your party theme. To help yourself find the right slant, start by thinking about your party objectives: are you looking to meet someone new, dance your socks off or celebrate an event, or all three? Potential ideas for parties with pros and cons include:

## Potluck parties

This is ideal and can cover a multitude of lazy tendencies. If you want lots of single men to arrive at your door, tell your friends they all have to bring one single man with them to gain entry; the idea being that all the single women then have a potluck chance of meeting someone new. The same principle can be applied to a dinner party (substituting the man for a food dish) if you don't want to cook.

**Pros:** less work for you.

**Cons:** guests will complain about the effort they have to put in.

## Cocktail parties

Forget the jazz and posh frocks (unless that's your thing) and tell everyone they have to make up a cocktail that represents something about them. Suggest you'll supply the basic alcohol and they have to bring their own special ingredients.

**Pros:** it will send a pre-party ripple of excitement through your guests.

**Cons:** you'll end up surrounded by many, many drunken people.

## 1960s/70s/80s parties

This is a good way to re-create a misspent youth or dress up without forcing your guests to spend a fortune on new clothes. It's worth noting these take more time to organise than most, thanks to the music and decoration aspect. Avoid at all costs if you can't be bothered to put in the work.

**Pros:** it takes care of all the music for the night.

**Cons:** it will put off anyone who hates 1960s/70s/80s music.

## *Karaoke parties*

If your idea of party heaven is serenading friends with your version of *I Will Survive*, this is the party for you. It's cheap and cheerful, as a karaoke machine can be hired for very little and guests flagging confidences can be fuelled with cheap bottles of beer.

*Pros:* it will have people laughing.

*Cons:* it will terrify a large percentage of your guests.

## *Surprise parties*

Again, maximum effort required on the organisation front as you have to persuade X amount of guests to keep the secret for X number of weeks. That's before you even think of what to do with the guest of honour while you're planning everything.

*Pros:* the guest of honour will love you forever.

*Cons:* you'll have a nervous breakdown before the day is through.

## *Baby and wedding showers*

If you've never experienced one of these, they are usually 4.00 p.m. drinks-and-food parties based around the bride or mum to-be. Best done with an all-female cast and gifts. Aim to make it a teatime treat of fancy cakes, small sandwiches and chocolates.

*Pros:* you'll feel very *Sex in the City*.

*Cons:* you'll be bored by the baby and wedding talk.

## Dinner parties

If you're a lazy cook, never opt for a party of more than six people, because the chances are, apart from the fact you won't have enough chairs or plates to go round, you won't enjoy it. Most importantly, always be realistic about your culinary expertise and never ever try a dish you haven't cooked or a recipe that includes ingredients you've never heard of.

*Pros:* throwing a dinner party will score big brownie points and will make up for all the times you've been invited over to dinner.

*Cons:* you have a lot to live up to.

## Catered parties

These can be held at local venues, clubs and/or restaurants and are basically fabulous for the lazy girl because all you have to do is pay for someone to do all the hard work. However, they are slightly more stressful than most, as you have to ensure a certain amount of people turn up on the night and don't destroy the place.

*Pros:* easy work for you.

*Cons:* expensive bills for you.

## Offbeat themed parties

These are fancy dress parties with a theme, and work because they get your guests thinking and talking, and all the men won't come as James Bond and all the women as Lara Croft. Dead celebrities, Stars in Your Eyes (in other words, come as your favourite pop star) and DJ parties, where everyone takes a turn trying to be an Ibiza club animal, are just some of the offbeat ideas that can make pretty good parties. The good thing about parties like these is it shows initiative, it makes your party memorable and it encourages people to mix and take part. However, when thinking about the right party theme, always take your guests into account. If you happen to know a bunch of extroverts, you can get away with pretty much anything. Otherwise keep it simple and non-tacky (unless it's tacky as a theme, of course). Colour-themed parties are also a little hard to do – and look revolting on the food front (who wants to eat blue pizzas?).

*Pros:* guaranteed laughs.

*Cons:* hard work for you.

## Murder mystery parties

Here's one for the fancy dress fans who may be feeling a little sidelined by this chapter. Murder mystery parties are basically dinner parties with a themed twist. Each guest gets a card as an invitation, inviting them to be a particular character in a murder story. Everyone then comes to dinner as that character and tries to work out who the murderer is through the actions and stories of the other guests. If you're feeling creative you can organise this yourself, or buy a murder mystery game from any game shop.

**Pros:** it gets people talking (even the shy).

**Cons:** it feels a little contrived.

# *Invitations*

If your party is in competition with a zillion other parties (for example it's a New Year event) then be sure to let your guests know well in advance of the date so you don't end up partying alone. Always back up verbal invitations with reminders of the time, the day, and whether or not guests should be expecting food and drink. If you're bothered by etiquette in any form whatsoever it's worth noting that parties that start at 7.00 p.m. should have food. However, food can mean anything from ready-made snacks to full-on gourmet delights. Also, note that if you mention food on the invitations people will expect more than crisps and dips.

Next, get your facts straight. Don't be the person who thinks they are having a party on Saturday 10th but writes 'Saturday' on the invitation, as guests will be turning up all month.

## The info

Things your guests want to know from your invitation:

- What's happening – that is, why are you having a party?
- When the whole event is going to take place and where – believe it or not this is the one point people forget to make clear on invitations.
- What time it is all going to start. This is essential if you need people to arrive by a certain time; for example, if it's a surprise party or dinner party.
- What to wear – only important if there's a dress code at a venue you've hired or if it's a party where you want people to make an effort.
- What to bring – a person, a bottle, a dish, a present and so on.
- What not to bring – also important if you don't want to end up with extra people you can't fit in and if, for some reason, you don't want gifts.
- How to RSVP. It sounds formal but it's better to know who can make it and who can't in terms of space issues well before the day of your party.
- What time your party is going to finish. You may not know this if it's an informal house party, but if it's at a venue it's good to tell your guests that they will all be kicked out at 11.00 p.m.

# Issue impressive invitations

No, this is not a TV moment where I tell you how to laminate toilet-roll style invitations in gold leaf but the place where I mention it pays to make your invitation memorable. This is because technology has created more and more ways to issue an invitation, and if you send out something bland, the chances are your guests won't even notice they've been invited and so won't turn up.

## Email

This is a seemingly brilliant and cheap way to send out invitations. However, if you are sending out a round-robin email to 40 people and asking them to reply, you will be bombarded with emails at work all day. This is also a good way to end up with 800 people, as invitees start forwarding your email to friends, chatrooms and work colleagues. If you're going to choose this route, it's better to send personal emails to 40 people.

*Pros:* it's fast and cheap.

*Cons:* it could turn into the latest Internet chain invitation.

## Text

A somewhat abrupt way to issue an invite, which also screams informal. This is fine if your party is informal, but not so fine if it's a red carpet event. Texting is great if you don't have much to say besides 'Turn up at 8.00 p.m.'.

*Pros:* fast and simple.

*Cons:* expensive and easy to misread.

## Paper invitations

Having invitations printed is an expensive route to go down unless it's a very formal event. You can, however, be creative with how you do it. One friend pockets piles of free postcards from pubs and sticks invitations on the back to send out. Another does the same with playing cards and beer mats. Balloons can also work (though obviously don't blow them up before sending), as do condoms (new ones, not used ones) if you want to be cheeky. Other ideas include matchboxes (again free from bars and restaurants) and money from Monopoly sets.

*Pros:* looks flash and creative.

*Cons:* you have to buy stamps.

## Word of mouth

This is great if you have a good memory and terrible if you don't. Are you capable of keeping track of who you've told

*tip*

Look for errors on your invitations. Before you send them, get a good friend (with an eye for detail) to look them over, because the chances are there will be something you've missed out.

and who you haven't? Can you even remember what you said after three pints on Saturday night?

*Pros:* it's the cheapest option.

*Cons:* people will forget what you've said to them.

## Invitation dos and don'ts

Do invite more than the required number of people.
Don't invite everyone and his dog.

Do make the effort to write/email a proper invitation.
Don't just say, 'Pass the word along'.

Do be specific about time/place/event.
Don't be vague about the bits that are important to you.

Do make a list of people you want to invite, or else you'll forget someone important.
Don't invite people at the last minute because you're scared you won't have enough people.

# How to make throwing a party easier on yourself

## The essentials: drink and food, and utensils

Now you've laid the basics in place your biggest problem is time management. It's easy to think that getting a party together doesn't take much effort after the initial inviting and venue issues. However, ensuring you have enough drink, food, cutlery, glasses and even toilet roll means it pays to get organised.

'Prepare ahead' should be your mantra, because the more you can do before the event (that is the day before) the more you can relax on the day and the more you can party.

The best ways to throw a fantastic party on the cheap are:

- Go wholesale for your equipment, such as plastic cups, rubbish bags and plates. If that's not posh enough for you, hire your glasses from a local off-licence chain, or better still ask your friends to lend you plates and glasses (although this could prove expensive if they break).
- Don't be hung up on perfection. In a party anything goes (within reason), which means all your plates don't have to match, your glasses don't have to be cut glass and your booze the best money can buy.

- Buy your alcohol wisely. Litre bottles of sodas and colas are cheaper than cans. No-name brands are fine for orange juice and even spirits. With beer and wine, however, don't go cheap, as these do tend to be noticeably different.
- Ask your friends to bring a bottle, but state whether you want soft drinks, mixers, and beer or wine so you end up with a variety of drinks.
- Buy at least four corkscrews, because two are bound to go missing and you'll spend the whole night searching for something that will crack open the bottles of wine.
- Buy ice in packs from the off-licence and buy a plastic crate. Tip in the ice and load in a variety of bottles and cans; keep the rest in the fridge. This way you can regularly re-stock the drink rather than let your guests have a free-for-all in your cupboards.
- With foods, go for snacks that can be picked up and put in a napkin to avoid using cutlery and plates. Again, think basic: bread, cheese, dips, cut up and crudités (raw vegetables); things that can be done quickly and with zero kitchen effort from you.
- Also try to have a selection of hot and cold foods. This not only looks good but the smell will entice your guests to hang around and sample the goods. Choose ready-made party packs available from all large supermarkets.
- If you're no good at cooking, enlist your most culinary friends to help out. Friends like to feel helpful and involved, and won't feel taken for granted as long as you pay for the ingredients.
- Ask friends to help you move furniture, set out drinks and basically make life on the day a bit easier for you. Better still, set

them tasks so you're not still cutting up bread and sending
someone out for wine when the doorbell rings.

- Make/buy compilation tapes/mini-discs so that your CDs
  aren't being used as beer mats by the end of the night. Flatter
  a music-mad friend into taking control of this area so it isn't a
  free-for-all and your equipment doesn't get hammered.

# Decoration and location

You don't have to be Martha Stewart or the Queen to have
a fantastic-looking venue, but it pays to try. Clearing away
your clutter and baby pictures will not only impress your
guests but also save you from everyone getting to know
your intimate personal history. More importantly, it will
help create the right atmosphere, and what's a party without that? This means: pay attention to details.

Firstly, is there enough space for your friends to move
around or will they end up invading your bedroom and
sitting in the wardrobe? Work out what furniture needs to
stay and what should go. People need somewhere to sit
(not everyone, but enough space so they can have a rest if
they want to), but people also need space to dance, get a
drink and get to the bathroom.

At the same time, help make your post-party life easier
by clearing space in all rooms. This means: file away your
clutter so that the room looks bigger, and if it looks too

bare, fill places with flowers or pictures. If you're stuck on the decor front, think about what you're tying to create in each room. Do you want people to feel relaxed, hyped up, ready to dance or ready to sit and chat? Your decor should reflect the kind of party you're trying to have.

However, on the whole don't obsess too much about the finer details. Yes, you want to make your place look good but it doesn't have to resemble the Ritz to score interior design points from your friends.

## *Party lighting*

**Drinks parties:** medium to low background music, with lamp lighting and/or candles.

**Dance parties:** low lighting, medium to loud background music, little or no furniture.

**Cocktail parties:** medium lighting, good decor; think chic flowers and slow-paced background music.

# *Essential lazy decoration tips*

- Create the right atmosphere by turning off all overhead lights and light the room with fairy lights.

- Drape fairy lights over plants, around windows and mantelpieces for maximum effect.
- Avoid lit candles if you're having more than ten people and don't want your house to burn down.
- Avoid draping scarves over lamps; again, it's a major fire risk. Instead, change light bulbs to coloured bulbs for a soothing effect.
- Scatter flower petals on the food table and around plates.
- Place tea lights inside candle pots.
- Ask your most creative friend for design tips on how to do up your room, or scour interior magazines for ideas.
- While it pays to put away your most expensive ornaments, do keep part of your style in the room so guests feel as if they are at home.
- If you're at a venue, don't be afraid to make your mark on the room and/or insist on flowers, balloons or lighting while you're booking the event.
- Be careful about how to arrange food on plates. Effort makes a huge difference. Think: large platters, different colours of food on one plate, interesting mixes of cuisine and fruit.
- Finally, think like a guest: what would you like to see when you walk into a party? What would impress you/make you feel comfortable/make you think WOW!? This is what to aim for.

# 20 *ways*
## *to enjoy throwing a party*

**1  When stressed, delegate**
So, it's your party, this doesn't mean you have to do everything. If you're stuck for time, rope your best friends and family in to help. Better still, call up your most organised friend, and let her whip your party into shape.

**2  Don't feel responsible for your guests**
If you're worried about inviting someone who doesn't know anyone else, encourage them to bring a friend so you won't feel responsible for their enjoyment all night. And when introducing people to each other mention things they have in common and then scoot off and let them do the rest.

**3  Make your invitation exclusive**
Otherwise you're asking for an open house for all. Crowded parties look good on the surface but can annoy guests if they can't get to where the drinks are, hear each other above the music or move easily from room to room.

**4  Have your music suit the party**
You may like Metallica but if your party is a surprise do for someone else, choose music that suits them. Remember: music creates atmosphere – so what are you trying to say by your choice? Jazz/blues equals mellow; R&B says sexy; and disco and pop says dance!

**5  Always overestimate numbers**
This way you'll never be short of space, drink and food. There's nothing worse than having hungry, thirsty guests milling around your house searching your cupboards for sustenance.

**6  Keep things simple**
Party games, name tags and exotic flowers littering the tables can sound good fun but in reality can make people feel as if they are at a work function. Just get the basics in place – music, food and drink –

and let your guests have a good time on their own.

## 7 Think like a guest

Especially if you're stuck for what to stock your drinks table with and what to do about furniture. If you were going to someone else's party, what would you expect? What would you throw out? What would you find amazing? And what would make you go home early?

## 8 Think about yourself too

OK, enough about your guests – it's your party as well, so make sure there are elements you're going to enjoy. Is the music to your liking? Will you have time to dance/mingle and play the party goddess (instead of slaving over a hot oven)?

## 9 Create a party atmosphere

Most parties die an early death because the hosts don't even try to create a party vibe. To get guests instantly in the mood, turn the lights down, or use low-lighting bulbs and lamps. Make sure people can hear the music but aren't deafened by it, and make drinks accessible (and bins, otherwise it will take you a week to clear up).

## 10 Build on what you've started

This means: don't blast out all your dance favourites at the beginning of the night, start off slowly so people can feel themselves wanting to dance, rather than feeling pressurised to dance. Likewise, with the drink, start with mixers and build to shots and chasers unless you want all your guests drunk by 10.00 p.m.

## 11 Get your timings right

Unless you're specific about a time, no one will arrive at the stated time so don't panic. Starting at 8.00 p.m. means you can expect guests at about 9.00, with a second wave coming at around 10.00 p.m. If you live miles from anywhere, most of your guests will hotfoot it out of your place around midnight so they won't have to pay a fortune for a cab.

**12 When things go wrong...**
Don't panic! Parties rarely go to plan and that means you can expect hitches, such as forgetting to buy soft drinks for the drivers, running out of ice or realising all your guests are veggies when all you have are sausages. Relax – it's not the end of the world.

**13 Get your props in order**
This means if you are having a cocktail party make sure you have jugs, lots of ice and long glasses to mix everything in. If you're having a barbecue, ensure you have fuel/coals, as you'd be amazed at how many people forget that vital piece of equipment. To help, write a list of all the props you need to buy apart from the food and drink. This list should include post-party tidy-up props, too.

**14 Parties have a mind of their own**
If your dance party has turned into a stand-around-and-chat party, don't despair. Parties have a mind of their own and sometimes no amount of pushing in one direction will make a party go the way you want it to. If 90 per cent of your guests are happy, you should be too.

**15 Don't overestimate how much time you have**
No matter how organised you are, you can't do everything on the day of the party because (a) you'll be exhausted; and (b) you'll end up in a panic. Buy drink and decorations a week ahead. Buy food and select music three days ahead, clean your house and prepare some food a day ahead. Move furniture on the day, get ready two hours before and lay the drink out an hour before people arrive.

**16 Do a party sweep at the midway point**
This means swiftly trash up empties, old cups and wasted food and then lay out a fresh load of drink and food so guests don't start thinking the party is over. This is also a good time to change the tempo of the music, open windows for air (so your guests don't fall asleep) and break up cliques.

## 17 Protect your valuables

This doesn't mean your guests are going to steal your silver, but that things get broken. Make sure all your valuables (computer/TV/fragile ornaments) are placed in a room that you can lock, so people don't migrate there. If your party is all over your house, lock things away in a cupboard.

## 18 Make things easy for your guests

You may live quite happily in a house where there is no door or lock to the toilet but your guests won't be happy if they are caught with their knickers down. Likewise, be clear about where your party is. If your venue entails a long walk, warn your guests about shoes and umbrellas, and so on.

## 19 Make your guests feel special

Basically be in a good mood. Welcoming your guests with a smile rather than a panicked 'Oh-my-god-thank-goodness-you're-here' welcome will instantly relax your guests and make them feel glad they've come. Ensure you spend at least five minutes with each person throughout the night or else they'll feel like a filler guest and never come to one of your parties again.

## 20 Finally, relax

And enjoy yourself – because that's the whole point of throwing a party!

# chapter 2

# How to look good

It's an unfair fact of life that when you want to look glowing, glorious and gorgeous, you either wake up with a spot the size of Everest at the end of your nose and/or hair that would give your local chip shop a good run for its money! Given what you probably put your face, hair and skin through during the year, it's hardly surprising that you need a rescue plan for the party season.

## What is detoxing?

Detoxing is a spring-clean system akin to de-cluttering your house. This means you start by binning all the rubbish, tat and junk that is littering up your fridge and cupboards: the very stuff that also clogs up your digestive system and aids all of the above beauty meltdown symptoms. So, for a whole weekend, out go the following (and, yes, you do have to bin them or give them away, otherwise you'll give in to temptation sometime around 3.00 p.m. on Saturday afternoon):

## The pre-party detox

Answer yes, to three or more of the following and it's likely you need the pre-party detox to get your body and face into party shape:

- Does your skin have a spotty and vaguely grey pallor?
- Are you exhausted even when you first wake up?
- Is your tongue coated in a white, silver or yellowy-grey layer?
- Is your breath bad?
- Do your gums bleed or feel sensitive?
- Is your skin itchy?
- Are you suffering from headaches?
- Is your neck stiff?
- Is your stomach bloated?
- Are your nails broken and brittle?
- Is your hair lacklustre?
- Have spots become the bane of your life?
- Is your skin flaky and dry?
- Are your eyes surrounded by bags or red rimmed?
- Are your lips chapped?
- Is your body aching?
- Are you stuffed-up inside?

## Out goes ...

- Processed foods, such as crisps, ready-made meals, and cakes and biscuits – all heavy on the salt, fat and sugar front.
- Chocolate – it's laden in fat and sugar.
- Alcohol – it's heavy on calories and in sugar.
- Full-fat dairy – er ... full of fat!
- Fizzy drinks – they're full of calories, salt and sugar.
- Caffeine – it's full of stimulants that keep you artificially alert.
- Lounging about on the sofa – it does nothing for your well-being, if that's all you do.
- Late nights – go to bed an hour later than usual every night for a week, and by Sunday you'll have lost a whole night's sleep: cue fatigue, lack of concentration, bad circulation and a bad temper.

## In comes ...

- Water – and lots of it.
- Fresh fruit – good if you have a sweet tooth but also kind on your body.
- Green leafy vegetables – excellent detoxifiers and rich in anti-oxidants that help fight off pollutants in your body, such as the effects of a bad diet and alcohol.
- Lean meats and fish – they're rich in protein.
- Green tea – it's full of antioxidants to aid your detox.
- Nuts – they're rich in omega-3 essential fatty acids to help boost your immune system.
- Exercise – 30 minutes once a day will kickstart your energy levels.
- Eight hours sleep a night – they call it beauty sleep for a reason.

The point of all this is simply to give your organs a chance to have their own personal clear-out, leading to improved skin condition, more energy and better beauty all round. Do the detox correctly (see Party Detox Plan below) and not only will you feel better but you'll also look better. Even better news is a weekend detox is the easiest detox you can do and it won't kill you or make your skin erupt, and it's easier than you think to stick to (good news for lazy girls everywhere). For best results plan your detox weekend a week before a big event (also to avoid partying with detox spots), and in the week before keep to the main rules to ensure you keep all your good results.

## *Lazy girl toxins*

Where your toxins are coming from:

**Coffee and tea:** five to six cups a day can lead to caffeine toxicity which results in restlessness, dry skin and tiredness.
**Alcohol:** this is super-toxic and can lead to liver damage, heart strain and dehydration.
**Salt:** this definitely needs to be eliminated during a detox as it aids dehydration and causes bloating.
**Sugar:** again, it's essential to avoid sugar (in the form of chocolate and cakes) during a detox because it accelerates mood swings and headaches.
**Dairy:** these are mucus-forming foods that release toxins, which in turn cause sinus problems and skin complaints.

## *The detox rules*

As the main aim of a detox is to cleanse your body, you need to do two things: (1) remove old toxins; and (2) limit your intake of new ones.

So start by gradually easing yourself into the cleansing programme; that is, give up coffee a few days before your weekend, or else your body will retaliate with all kinds of strange noises and skin problems. Next, aim to follow a low-fat diet, rich in vegetables, and drink at least 1½ litres to 2 litres (3½ pints) of water a day (a glass every 45 minutes should do it) for at least two weeks to ensure you keep the benefits going for longer than your weekend.

When detoxing ensure that you:

1. Never detox if you are pregnant, breastfeeding, on medication, diabetic, have kidney or liver problems, or are ill.
2. Don't overdo it. Start slowly and always rest while you're detoxing. Partying and detoxing don't go hand in hand.
3. Enlist a group of friends to do it with you (misery does love company).
4. Make some effort to make the food you have to eat appetizing. Munching on broccoli spears isn't fun for anyone. Think stir-fries, steamed, flavours and so on.
5. Write down your three-day objectives before you begin, and when you feel your willpower flagging read your list.
6. Swap food goodies for beauty goodies. If you're staying in all weekend (in which case get an exercise video and do it once a

day) surround yourself with face masks, exfoliators, nail varnish, pedicure kits – anything to spoil your body with.

7. Drink the water you put aside, as the body needs this to help toxins exit quickly.

8. Make your bedroom an ideal rest area. Light candles, clear out all the clutter and make it a place you really do want to go and sleep in. A good sleep tip is to buy earplugs and an eye mask so that external light and noise won't wake you up.

## Big results for small changes

- Cut down on wheat. Most of us eat too much in our daily life. If you're a cereal/sandwich/pasta kind of girl, you could do with cutting wheat out entirely for two weeks and then slowly re-introducing it, so your system doesn't get over-loaded and bloated.
- Always pick brown over white when choosing bread, rice and pasta. Not only is it better for you nutritionally but also brown produce is less refined and so has less sugar and salt.
- Eat butter – yes, you read that right. Butter is better for you than margarine, as it has less trans-fats and is therefore healthier for your body.
- Don't fry foods – stir-fry by all means, grill, and better still bake or poach. You'll save yourself extra fat grams and cut your toxin levels.
- Buy organic – this is a detox essential, as most foods now come complete with a variety of chemicals and pesticides. If you can't be bothered to buy organic, make sure you rinse and wash food thoroughly.

# The party detox plan

### Day one

**Wake up:** start the day with a glass of warm water and lemon juice to flush out your system.

**Breakfast:** 45 minutes later eat a fresh fruit salad that contains at least three different fruits; one should ideally be pineapple, as it helps to cleanse the gut. Fruit is also an excellent start to the day as it helps activate the liver (the body's main cleansing organ), stimulate the bowel and gives you all the essential vitamins and minerals you need.

**Lunch:** make a salad with as much mixed raw vegetables and nuts as you want. Use olive oil on the salad. The enzymes in the raw vegetables will boost your metabolism and give you some much-needed energy, whereas the fibre will speed up the cleansing process. Add a small piece of lean protein – either tofu or fish.

**Snacks:** hungry? Then snack on grated carrots or apple slices, and drink plenty of water.

**Dinner:** aim to have your last meal of the day before 8.00 p.m. as this gives you plenty of time to digest food before going to sleep. Although raw is best, if you can't face

another salad, lightly steam some fresh vegetables or stir-fry them in a wok and season to taste. If you're starving, add a small piece of lean meat (no bigger than your palm), or have a bowl of vegetable soup with the stir-fry.

*Beauty treats:* buy an exfoliator and skin brush and give yourself a vigorous rub down prior to getting in the bath. You'll help shear off those dead skin cells and leave your skin radiant with health.

### Day two

*Wake up:* start the day with a glass of warm water and lemon juice to flush out your system.

*Breakfast:* have a bowl of stewed fruit (don't add sugar), a live bio yoghurt and a glass of fruit juice and herbal tea.

*Lunch:* have a chicken salad (don't use a rich creamy dressing but make one from oil and vinegar with garlic), or a tuna niçoise salad. Also make sure there are at least seven different vegetables in your salad besides lettuce (try cucumber, tomatoes, avocado, green beans, sweetcorn, red peppers, carrots and/or baby spinach).

*Snack:* eat a packet of unsalted almonds, or fruit such as apples and pears, or even a small tub of cottage cheese.

*Dinner:* eat roasted vegetables and brown rice. Vegetables should include broccoli, peppers, onions, potatoes, carrots and cauliflower, and can be seasoned with garlic, cayenne pepper, ginger and soy sauce.

*Beauty treats:* buy a face and hair mask relevant to your skin and hair type, plaster it on, place cucumber slices over your eyes, lie down and snooze for 15 minutes (set an alarm clock, just in case you nod off for the night). Wash off the face mask with a warm muslin cloth, to help with exfoliation, then liberally apply face moisturiser. Run warm water through your hair, comb it and leave it to dry naturally.

## Day three

*Wake up:* start the day with a glass of warm water and lemon juice to flush out your system.

*Breakfast:* make your own muesli (preferably the night before): add almonds, walnuts and hazelnuts to raw oats, cover with orange juice and leave in the fridge overnight (the mixture soaks up the juice). In the morning add a small pot of live bio yoghurt.

*Lunch:* have an open sandwich – double the filling and halve the bread. Use lean grilled chicken, mustard, a variety of roasted vegetables and a side salad of at least seven salad ingredients.

**Snack:** oatcakes and hummus (a tablespoon).

**Dinner:** eat a large bowl of vegetable soup, jacket potato with cottage cheese and an egg, plus a large side salad.

**Beauty treats:** give yourself a manicure and pedicure (see below), making sure you also spend time filing and shaping your nails and soaking your hands in warm water to help them soften. After applying polish, apply hand cream (or Vaseline – the lazy girl's best make-up tool) and lie on the sofa for an hour to let it sink in.

## The lazy girl way to detox

If you've by-passed all of the above as too much bother but still want to reap the benefits of detoxing, then there is a sneaky way round. Here's the way to get some of the benefits with half the effort.

### If you do only one detox thing

Drink water and lots of it. Water is a girl's best friend in more ways than one, as not only does it help flush out toxins but it also keeps you hydrated; meaning, less fatigue, less yawning and less bad-tempered days. If you

## Reactions to detoxing

During the detox diet there may be some side effects to look out for:

**A headache** triggered by the release of toxins from the body. Drink more water.

**Bad breath** caused by toxins being expelled. A good tip is to rinse your mouth with hot water and lemon juice and/or scrape your tongue with a teaspoon.

**Spots;** if you get an outbreak, or your skin becomes dry, don't panic, it will go within two days.

**Fatigue;** don't reach for the aspirin or a coffee, just curl up and relax – it won't last beyond 24 hours.

hate the taste or lack of taste, spruce it up with lemon, and lime, or ginger.

### If you take only one vitamin

Make it a multi-vitamin with minerals: one pill, a hundred times the benefit. Ideal if you're someone who also eats badly, cheats on sleep and feels constantly on the brink of a cold.

### If you avoid only one food

Make sure it's refined sugar found in junk food, processed foods, and cakes and biscuits. This is the stuff that bloats you, makes you feel tired and leads to blood sugar highs and lows, and constant chocolate cravings.

### If you can do only one beauty thing

Make sure you get enough sleep. Cheat on the snooze front and you're asking for beauty problems of the grey-skin kind.

### If you do only one active thing

Make it walking. Get into the habit of walking instead of driving and taking the bus, and not only will you tone up your legs, thighs and bottom but also you will burn calories and improve your breathing technique.

### If you have to have one drink

Make it an Ocean Breeze – cranberry, grapefruit and vodka. Cranberry is excellent for the urinary tract, grapefruit is rich in good stomach enzymes and vitamin C, and vodka is low in sugar as it's one of the purest forms of alcohol.

### If you give up only one thing

Make it cigarettes. Apart from causing the obvious, smoke literally gets in your skin and hair leaving your skin a nicer shade of grey, your hair lacklustre, and makes your breath stink!

# 'Tis the time to be gorgeous Part 1: pre-party beauty prep

## Skin

Whether you have dry, oily or combination skin, if you want smouldering looks, all you have to do is avoid the five deadly sins of skincare:

1. Never apply make-up over broken spots.
2. Never apply foundation to just your face.
3. Never take your skin for granted (also known as: wear sunscreen).
4. Never apply new make-up over old.
5. Never forget to moisturise.

Even the laziest beauty girl should be able to do the above, simply because it's a guaranteed way to have healthy-looking

## tips

Now you're in tiptop shape on the inside, it's time to focus on the outside. The joy of a good beauty regime and wearing liberal doses of make-up is it literally does cover a multitude of sins, including bad skin, lank hair and spotty faces. If you're about to head out, here's all you need to do to ensure total party-goddess status.

skin, as well as maintaining party skin that doesn't have people peering at your face for all the wrong reasons.

If, however, you want to look good all year round and can only afford one product, make it a great face cream (and 'great' doesn't necessarily mean horribly expensive or designed by an astronaut), as this will help your make-up go on smoothly, giving you some fake radiance and, more importantly, keep your skin baby-soft.

A good face cream will not only help attract water to your skin and hold it there but will also be a cream that you can apply easily and one that doesn't cause your skin to tingle or your make-up to separate. When choosing a cream, always ask for a small tester; go home, try it out and then come back and buy it if it works. Don't naturally assume you know your skin type or opt for the anti-ageing pot (if you're under 30 you don't need it, and if you're over 30 you still may not need it). Remember: different creams work for different people, and expensive isn't always the better option.

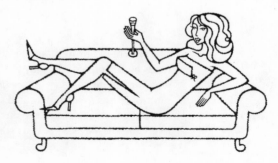

## Ingredients to look out for

**AHAs** are also known as alpha hydroxy acids. These are fruit acids that work by boosting the exfoliating process. They work well on normal and combination skins but are too harsh for dry and sensitive skins.

**Ceramides** are said to work on a cellular level and help the skin by supporting the structure and trapping moisture. They are usually found in anti-ageing creams.

**Liposomes** apparently go further into the outer layer of the skin than any other type of cream, allowing your moisturiser to go deeper and giving you softer skin.

**SPF**, or sun-protection factor. Not strong enough for the summer but fine to protect you in the winter.

### Spots

A spot usually occurs not because you pigged out on chips and chocolate but because the sebaceous glands, which are responsible for producing sebum (oil) for the skin, go into overproduction and clog up skin pores, leaving the pore to become inflamed with bacteria. This usually happens when you're stressed or when your period is due. Rather than hide your head under a pillow for two weeks, here's how to deal with the nasty blighters.

## The party spot survival guide

If a spot the size of Everest is erupting on your nose, here's how to cover up.

1. If the spot is ready to burst, you can pick it. Use a tissue and pull the skin apart (rather than together) and don't squeeze so hard that you damage the skin.
2. Now place a clean tissue with antiseptic cream on the spot and apply pressure for a minute to allow the spot to start to heal (less than a minute and it will still be weeping).
3. Now allow two hours for the spot to dry completely, otherwise make-up will either infect your skin or sit on top of the spot.
4. When dry apply a dab of foundation and even out with a sponge. When that is dry add powder and leave to settle. If the powder sits on top, dust off the remainder with a brush.
5. Stop looking at it and trying to improve the look, you'll just make it worse.

### Serious treatments

(For those nasty spots that never seem to go away.)

#### Try a medicated response

While there are no overnight cures, over-the-counter products can help. Give each product you use an eight-week chance, and if you don't see an improvement after

# *tip*

If you're going to squeeze a spot before you go out, make sure you do it at least two hours before you start putting your make-up on, so it has time to dry.

that try something new. Look for products containing benzoyl peroxide – an oxidising agent that will act against blackheads by causing your skin to peel and reducing bacteria on the skin. Or try a product with azelaic acid; this unblocks clogged-up hair follicles and also loosens blackheads.

### Try laser treatment

The N-Lite Laser is the biggest breakthrough for spots in years. Apart from being painless and non-invasive, the treatment gets rid of acne for good. This is because the laser light kills the bacteria that causes acne and then the collagen-building laser helps create the formation of new collagen around the area of the spot, leading to healthier skin and less breakouts.

### See your GP

If over-the-counter products don't work for you, see your GP for oral antibiotics or even the pill (certain brands can help with acne). Or ask for a referral to a dermatologist.

## Lips

Use a lip balm at least once a week. These are designed to protect, soothe and seal the lips, helping them to remain moist and supple. For juicy party lips that look and feel kissable, mix lipstick with Vaseline and apply with a brush.

## Eyes

The problem with eyes is that the skin under the eyes is very delicate and fine, which means it's not only prone to lines but is also the first place to highlight a hangover and lack of sleep.

### Red and painful eyes

A lack of vitamin A can cause the eye's natural secretions to dry up, making the eyes red and painful. Beta-carotene found in vitamin A (carrots, apricots) is a powerful antioxidant and will help protect the eye from smoky environments and sunlight.

### Dark circles

These can be hereditary but tend to become more noticeable as you age and your skin loses its natural firmness. Lack of sleep also encourages this look, as blood rushes into the blood vessels causing that shadowy look. The best cure is, simply, regular sleep. To help aid this try chamomile tea. Apart from encouraging good sleep, chamomile helps reduce facial tension and therefore reduces the formation of dark circles.

### Bags under your eyes

While nothing can get rid of bags for good (save plastic surgery) you can help reduce that puffy look with one of the following: cucumber slices, cold teabags, and ice wrapped in a flannel. For more permanent solutions cut down on salt in your diet as this can also cause your bags to inflate.

## Hair

Having a bad hair day? Worried it's going to ruin your perfectly planned party? If so, it's time for some last-minute party hair ideas. Firstly, it's worth knowing you can actually get away with more than you think when it comes to hair. Here's how:

### Greasy hair

Left it too late to wash your hair? All is not lost. The lazy way to shock your hair into shape is to blast your roots with cold air from your hairdryer. Not only does this lift the roots and give you instant bounce but it also equals less hair fussing all round.

*tip*

If your hair is greasy owing to excess product (too much serum, conditioner or spray) then wash it through with vodka – yes, you read that right. Vodka is pure alcohol and will take all that sticky stuff right out, leaving your hair cleaner. Be sure to wash it through with your normal shampoo and conditioner or else you'll reek of eau d'alcohol all night long.

### Frizzy hair

Sorry, but frizzy hair is usually the result of bad hair treatment. To calm the wild look instantly, use a little conditioner or balm, no bigger than a ten pence coin, rub it through your hands, and then smooth it on to the ends.

Products that contain panthenol or silicone-based products add smoothness and shine, BUT use too much and your hair will look lank.

Conditioners with a lighter touch include those with shea butter and seed oils; these also seal the cuticles, erasing frizz and leaving you with either sexy celebrity curls or hair straighter than straight. As for blow-drying – help yourself by pointing your hairdryer downwards as it blows, so that the hair lies flat.

### Dry hair

Hair that is dry is hair that is dying for a drink. To hydrate it just feed it moisture, this means less shampoo (which can dry hair out) and more conditioner, preferably one that you can leave in. Also watch how you dry your hair. Overall, practise gentleness when styling. Do not brush hair when it's wet (it causes hair to break). Use a de-tangler if you are combing wet curly hair; let hair dry naturally for five to ten minutes before styling; and, finally, get a trim every six weeks.

# Nails

Are your hands letting you down? If your nails are brittle, broken and/or chewed, here's how to save them.

### Ridged nails

The nail plate is made up of three layers and when you accidentally bash your nails, or trap them in a car door you'll find yourself with uneven waves across your nail. In most cases ridged nails are actually hereditary and the best way to improve the look of the nail is to keep your nails short and buff down the ridges with a nail buffer. A buffer looks like an emery board but it has three different surfaces. You buff with each of them to create a smooth nail plate, but only do this twice a month or you'll damage the nail.

### White spots

There's a multitude of reasons for the appearance of white spots, including, say some experts, a lack of calcium and zinc. However, in most cases bruising the nail plate is to blame, caused by knocking the nail. The best action is to leave the marked nail to grow itself out. However, if you're plagued with white spots, go down the preventative route and be aware of how you treat your hands. Nasty bangs and drumming your nails can damage the nail plate and cause the very spots you're trying to rid yourself of.

## Feet

Soaking, buffing, massaging and polishing your poor old feet can be as good for the soul as it is for your soles. Not only does it feel great but it will also help you to stay on your feet for longer in high heels (mass party plus), and it will make a sexy strappy sandal look even sexier.

Getting yourself a pedicure or visiting a chiropodist is the number-one foot tip. While you can primp, pamper and polish at home, only a seasoned professional can cut your nails properly, shave off hard skin and get rid of corns – the backbeat to any sexy foot!

### Manicure essentials

If you are going to go it alone, arm yourself with:
- A pumice stone
- A nail buffer
- Cuticle oil and sticks
- Base coat and polish
- Cotton buds and varnish remover
- A rich skin cream with lanolin

Start by cutting nails straight across to avoid ingrown nails. Next, soak your feet in warm soapy water for ten minutes, and then gently use the pumice stone on the toughened areas of your feet. Now, take your feet out, dry properly

(make sure you get between your toes) and smother in body cream, being sure to rub into the nail area and ball of the feet (the place where high heels will hurt the most).

To work on your nails, apply the cuticle oil and then gently push back the cuticles with sticks. Your next step is to wipe the nails with polish remover and then apply the base coat and polish. If you suffer from wobbly hand, use a cotton bud to tidy up around the edges. Allow to dry fully (a good excuse to lie on the sofa for half an hour with your legs up – great for lymphatic drainage), and you're ready to go.

## Make-up tips for the uninitiated

For dramatic eyes, luscious lips and a flawless complexion you don't need a skipful of make-up, two hours and a trip to the beauty salon. It does help if you practise a good beauty routine of cleansing, moisturising and sunscreen, and it does help if you eat something healthy now and again. However, if you are a lost cause on all those fronts and you learn only one thing from this chapter, here's the section to read and pin on your mirror.

### The lazy girl essential basics

The make-up rules every girl should know before they slap it on:

- Your personality, not fashion should dictate your look.
- Blue eyeshadow does not look good on everyone; neither do red lipstick and overplucked brows.

- Less is always more with make-up – less of everything will give you more of a sexy look!
- Spidery eyelashes caked in mascara do not make your eyes look larger.
- Foundation should go beyond the jawline.
- Concealer will not cover up a large spot effectively.
- Make-up should always be put on near a good light but not underneath one.
- Expensive make-up is not necessarily better make-up.

### The lazy girl essential make-up tools

If all else fails, your fingers will do (clean ones please), but the following will help give you more of a professional glow:

- Tweezers
- Tissues
- Make-up sponge/brushes
- Eye make-up remover
- Cotton buds
- Baby lotion (good for moisturising and as a make-up remover)

### Lazy girl essential make-up

You don't need a make-up bag the size of a truck to look good. If you want good make-up on the cheap consider the following:

**A *powder/foundation mix in a compact*** goes on more easily, takes half the time of applying powder and foundation separately, and takes away the shine. Always test it first and walk into natural light to check out the colour. Do not believe shop assistants who say the colour is perfect.

**A *good lipstick*** that applies colour evenly. Always try it on your lips. Wipe the tester with a tissue first (unless you want to catch something) then apply with your finger by dabbing or dotting it on to your lips. Press your lips together to smooth out the colour, and then go outside the shop and have a look at the colour.

**A *concealer*** should be the same colour as your skin or else it will just highlight a blemish. As before, test for colour on a blemish/scar or on top of your cheekbone near your eye.

**A *pot of Vaseline*** is perfect to mix with lipstick to get that gloss look. Perfect also for smoothing down brows and dry bits and great to take off your make-up with. It is even good as mascara – use it to elongate the ends of your lashes.

### The plucking guide
Are you over-plucked or a meet-in-the-middle type of girl? Whatever your current look, it's worth noting that eyebrows have the power to transform your face, make your

eyes look larger and get you noticed. If you've never had your brows plucked before it's always worth visiting a professional to give yourself a line to work with. If you do go down that route, make sure you're firm with the plucker about the look you want (it's OK to take pictures with you) or else you may come out with a nearly naked look. The other pointer to be aware of before plucking is, like your legs, once you start messing with your brows, you have to keep going.

## The lazy girl's plucking guide

Buy flat-slant tweezers, as these are best for catching hold of the fine hairs. To judge whether you have the perfect tweezers, close them; they should meet quite tightly.

1. Stand under a bright light and have a good look at your brows. Your aim is to tidy up your natural line (not create a whole new one).
2. Pluck the bottom row first, one hair at a time, along the line of your arch.
3. Stand back, smooth down your brow and see if you need to do a second line.
4. Remove stray hairs between the brows. If in doubt about how much to take off, be conservative. This is one area where it's better to have more than less.

### *Foundation advice*

This is the number-one area where people go astray. Why? Well simply because they leave tidemarks around their face and don't bother to smooth the colour they are applying on to their neck. In reality your foundation should never be so dark that someone next to you can notice the change of colour from neck to face. However, if you are going for a more 'sun-kissed' look, help yourself by:

1. Applying your foundation with a sponge for a more even all-over look.
2. Next, pat it on to the skin, don't rub it in like cream, and remember to do your forehead, the hollows of your nose and around your brow area.
3. Before the foundation sets, apply powder with a brush lightly over your face and then dust off the excess.
4. If you don't have a brush, place a tissue over your face and lightly press against your skin to take off the excess.

### Getting lippy

Lipstick is another area where we all tend to go a little wild. Contrary to popular belief, lashings of red gloop backed up with gloss, does not make a man want to get up close and personal with you. To get the best look, you don't have to do that whole lip-liner, three-coats, blot-and-gloss number, instead try:

1. Making sure your lips aren't chapped first. If so, lightly exfoliate them with a small piece of rock salt and some water. Then apply lip balm/Vaseline.
2. Next, making sure your lips are dry, apply your lipstick either from the tube or with your finger.
3. Darker colours will make your lips look thinner, so use a colour as close to your natural colour as possible.
4. For a double colour/shine look, mix your lipstick with Vaseline and/or balm first.
5. Better still, after you've put your lipstick on, blot once with a tissue and apply a dab of balm to the centre of your lips, and you're ready to go.

### Eye-catching stuff

This can be the trickiest area to do, so if you're not adept at sultry eyeliner lines and fancy twirls of the mascara brush, don't be too ambitious with your make-up.

1. With mascara, you need only two coats at the most. Any more and you're back to that clumpy, spidery look. Apply to the top

lashes and leave to dry and then apply one coat to the lower lashes (if you need it).

2. With eye shadow don't go pinky, pearly and sparkly unless you have light-coloured eyes or want to make a statement. Best options are semi-matt with a colour close to your eye colour to emphasise your eyes.

3. Place a tissue under your eyes to stop the powder falling on to your cheeks.

4. Eyeshadow should sweep outwards to the hairline but never go further out than your eyebrows. Beware of going all over your eyelids if you never usually wear heavy eye make-up. Finally, blend, blend, blend ... so it doesn't look as if you've just smeared it across your eyes (use your ring finger to do this as it will apply less pressure than your forefinger).

5. Eyeliner is only a must if you know how to do it and have a steady hand; never rub your eyes. Beware the panda look.

# 'Tis the time to be gorgeous Part 2: pre-party clothes prep tips

The good news is – this is not the bit where I tell you what to wear, because the big plus of going to a party is that there are no rules. It's probably the one time where you can pretty much get away with looking outrageous, wear every colour under the sun and even go out in your underwear.

However, there are some lazy tips that can help you discover the stylist within, especially if you're the kind of girl who stands in front of her mirror and wails, 'I've got nothing to wear' or breaks down in sobs at her reflection.

## *Step one: stop judging yourself so harshly*

OK, so you have a few lumps and bumps. Your breasts stick out too far or don't stick out at all. Your stomach's too fat, or your bum's too flat and your clothes don't look right. If you're wearing the right size (avoid clothes, which are too baggy or too tight) your clothes will look just fine.

If you hate what you see, then you either have body issues (if so go to Chapter 3) or unrealistic expectations of what you should look like (if the name of a celebrity comes to mind, give yourself a hard slap).

Although this isn't the self-esteem pep talk section, learn to give yourself a break. Firstly, if you're trying to model yourself after someone famous, it's worth noting that they have a team of hairdressers, stylists and make-up artists all working on them, whereas you don't. Secondly, if you're living in the past or future, thinking of the time (or a time) when you looked or will look 'perfect' – GIVE IT UP! Live in the present and learn to deal with how you look now. The world is full of imperfection (thank God) and the sad truth is everyone else is too busy worrying about their own lumps and bumps to care about yours, so, basically, stop complaining and get dressed!

### Step two: invest in some good underwear

Throwing on an expensive outfit over greying, baggy and basically dilapidated underwear is akin to papering crumbling walls with £200 wallpaper. Meaning, the structure underneath will basically destroy the look on top. If your cups spillith over, the back of your bra rides up and your straps are always at your elbows, you have the wrong size on. A well-fitted bra is one that sits flat against your ribcage (the part between your boobs should lie flat), has straps that stay put and displays no bulges around the edges, back or front. Take a look at yourself in front of the mirror. If this isn't the case, go and get measured (any major department store will do this for you).

Secondly, if your knickers ride up your bottom, drop down from your hips and bag around the bottom, they are useless and need to be thrown away. Buy a size that fits you, not a size you wish you'd fit into or a pair you and your best friend could fit into together. And while you're at it, think about the style. G-strings do not look attractive on everyone, and old granny pants with steel-enforced panels are not necessary just because you have a little flab going around your middle.

*tip*

Seventy-five per cent of women wear the wrong bra size. So make sure you get fitted by a professional at your local department store.

## Step three: locate your natural shape

Speaking of granny knickers, rather than trying to squeeze, pummel and force yourself into clothes that restrict and bind you, always try to work with your natural shape (this is the body shape you are naturally meant to be). This will not only help you to feel more comfortable in your clothes but also help you to choose clothes that flatter your body:

**Vata/ectomorph:** if you are a vata type, you are likely to be slim with long legs and arms, and relatively bony.

**Pitta/mesomorph:** you're likely to be of medium build, and have moderate to low body fat. Often you'll be pear shaped with hips larger than your shoulders, and your legs the same length as your torso.

**Kapha/endomorph:** you have a curvy, softer and wider body. You're also likely to be of average height. Your legs are shorter than your torso, and your breasts tend to be larger than average.

## Step four: be brave with your clothes

What are you trying to say with your clothes? Femme fatale/man-eater/sex machine/girl who hides behind yucca all night? Whether you like it or not, clothes do maketh the woman, which means your clothes will often say more than you want them to. It's a party, which means it's a good time to take yourself out of your comfort zone and make an impact.

If you're usually found in trainers, try small heels. If you're a jean wearer, pull on a skirt or a dress. If you never bare your flesh, go sleeveless for the night. If you always wear black, try a hint of colour. Small changes can make a large impact. If you're completely stuck for what to do, ask your best friend or a friend whose dress sense you admire for a mini-makeover (natural stylists will always have an idea of what you should be doing).

## Step five: bling-bling effect

Finally, as the whole idea of a party is to let yourself shine, work out what your special 'bling-bling' factor will be. Usually this is the part of your own body you admire the most (if you can't find one, go back to Step One and read it through again). This is the part you should accentuate to its fullest.

If it's your hair, think style, shine, clips and sparkly bits. If it's your décolletage (your neckline) and face, use jewellery to help draw attention up and down. With legs, simple things like high heels, moisturiser with a shimmer, and sexy tights can pull them to everyone's attention. If it's your curves, wear well-fitted clothes that show off your sexy bits. Then take one last look in the mirror and go out and stop thinking about how you look!

# 20 *pre-party beauty tips*

**1 Think about your hidden bits**
You may look good on the surface, but if your hair crinkles to the touch, your feet scratch the floor and your hands are as soft as nails, you'll destroy the look. The aim is to soothe and soften – exfoliate and moisturise.

**2 Relax**
Stress can make you look as if you've run a marathon, have PMS and have never carried out a beauty procedure in your life. If you're prone to anxiety before an event, relax! Take regular time-outs not just for your mind, but for your looks too.

**3 Don't trowel on the make-up**
Cake it on in the pursuit of a flawless complexion and you'll end up looking as if you're trying to hide something or applying for a drag queen job. The idea is to enhance the kind of make-up you'd usually wear, not have a complete makeover.

**4 Avoid lipstick on your teeth**
Horrible beauty disaster, but easy to avoid. Simply apply your lipstick and then put your forefinger in your mouth and wrap your inner lips around it and drag your finger out. It will remove the colour only from the inside of your lips.

**5 Pass the daylight test**
Do you pass the daylight test? That is, how close to your skin colour is that foundation you're applying so liberally and how natural is that ruby-red lip gloss? Help yourself by putting make-up on in natural light, not by a bright mirror light. By a window (but not in the sun's glare) is best.

**6 Too much make-up?**
If your look looks too heavy and you've no time, get some tissues and gently press them against your skin to blot (not wipe) off excess lipstick, eye-shadow and foundation. Then take

another look and whatever looks the heaviest, take off and reapply.

## 7 Smooth out smudged nails
Either dip your finger in nail-polish remover very quickly – the colour will then even out on it's own – or wipe off and reapply two thin coats. Never apply another coat on top of the smudge or else it will look lumpy.

## 8 Be careful with fake tans
They can make you look great but always apply two nights before so you don't look orange on the night.

## 9 Avoid overspraying
Too much perfume will have people wincing in your presence. Spray on your neck, over your hair and top up four hours later.

## 10 Discoloured nails
An easy solution is to either remove your nail polish every night and/or use a base coat to protect the nail from discolouration. If it's too late for that, wipe over them with lemon juice and then buff. After buffing always ensure you use a protection layer (base- or top-coat) before applying new colour.

## 11 Don't try anything new the night before
Sunbeds, fancy facials, new scrubs and face masks may sound like a good pre-party idea but they are not. If you want to do a beauty treatment, do it 48 hours before a party to give your skin time to settle down.

## 12 Use concealer sparingly
Dab it on with your finger (never rub on) and avoid the temptation to keep adding to it, or else you'll just turn a small spot into a mountain of concealer.

## 13 Go easy on the rouge
Red cheeks either look healthy and defined or, at the worst, drag queen-like. To get them right, dip the brush in, blow off excess powder and then sweep across the cheekbones moving upwards.

## 14 A sneaky plucking tip

If you are plucking and you come across a really stubborn hair, put some concealer on the end of the tweezers. It really helps to get a grip and you'll yank it out with no trouble.

## 15 Spot cover extra

To mask big spots, use an opaque (a dense colour as opposed to a light one) concealer and apply with a foundation sponge (bought at any chemist).

## 16 Avoid face scrubs with rough ingredients

To be kind to your skin, use ordinary porridge oats. Take a handful and mix with water, and then rub on to your skin and wash off.

## 17 Muslin – a girl's best friend

Buy cheap squares at your local baby shop. They are fab to use as an exfoliating method to get rid of old skin cells, cheaper than cotton wool (as you can re-use them) and work well when it comes to make-up removal.

## 18 Close your pores

Or at least make them look closed. After you wash your face, run an ice cube over it to constrict the pores, then use an oil-controlling product beneath your moisturiser and foundation.

## 19 Don't forget your sense of smell

Be sure not to ruin the whole party look, and always apply a strong antiperspirant. Shave your armpits (as hair can make BO worse as it traps bacteria) and/or use an antibacterial soap in the shower.

## 20 It won't kill you to be lazy post-party

Sleeping in your make-up isn't a huge beauty no-no (once in a while). Make-up can sit quite happily on your face all day and won't ruin your complexion if it stays on all night occasionally; although, not so good for that first look in the bathroom mirror next morning.

# chapter 3

# *The little black dress plan*

If you're an ardent lazy girl, your good intentions to get fit for an event, be it a milestone birthday or a 'make-my-ex-jealous' party have probably been lost in a haze of late nights and pizza boxes. While it's tempting to think that the answer now only lies in a starvation diet and granny knickers, a better option lies in the lazy girl's four-week Little Black Dress Plan.

While this plan won't turn you into a supermodel (and let's face it, only plastic surgery ever will) it will help you trim down and tone up. Better still, as it lasts only a month even the most uncommitted (read: lazy) person will be able to make it work for them.

To drop a dress size, make sure you do the fitness plan and eating plan at the same time (or it will take double the time, if not longer). Both are designed to work together, and as this is only a four-week plan it won't kill you even if you're the laziest person in the world. How do we know? Because we tested it!

# The 'get-me-into-that-dress' eating plan

## The key pointers

- Eat unlimited amounts of vegetables and salad – the greener and leafier the better (but, sorry, no potatoes). Don't fry them, or add butter, or drown them in olive oil and salad dressing.
- Drink 2 litres (3½ pints) of water a day, and diet drinks, tea and coffee (with skimmed milk, but skip the cappuccinos). Avoid all fruit juices for the first two weeks; after that dilute with water.
- Meat, fish, eggs and low-fat cheeses are all allowed.
- No bread, pasta, rice or potatoes for the first two weeks. Don't panic, after that you can introduce them again.
- Avoid fruit for the first two weeks.
- Avoid the olive oil and low-fat trap. Yes, olive oil is healthier than other oils, but it's still oil.
- No alcohol for two weeks, and then you can start again.
- No processed meals, no chocolate, cakes, biscuits, crisps or junk food for four weeks.

## Menus

If you can't be bothered to think up your own menus, you can choose from the list below, which are all low fat and low calorie. If you're someone who buys all her meals ready made, always check labels for fat and sugar content before you buy. Try not to exceed 1,500 calories a day, and make sure your fat levels don't exceed 50g (2oz) a day.

### Breakfast (choose one a day)

- Scrambled eggs and two rashers of grilled bacon.
- A sausage with two fried eggs.
- Scrambled eggs, mushrooms, tomatoes and smoked salmon.
- Mushrooms, tomatoes, two poached eggs and bacon (grilled).
- One-hundred per cent rye bread (no wheat) and two boiled eggs.
- Omelette filled with low-fat cheese and two slices of ham.
- Poached eggs, grilled mushrooms and tomatoes.

### Lunch (choose one a day)

- Lean chicken (without skin) and vegetables, and a mixed green salad with balsamic vinegar.
- Grilled fish with salad made from lettuce, tomatoes, cucumber, mushrooms, avocado and carrots.
- Mozzarella and tomatoes, ½ dessert spoon of olive oil, with grilled chicken and vegetables.
- A pepper stuffed with roasted vegetables and cheese (add two boiled eggs if you didn't have them for breakfast).

- Small can of tuna, prawns (or seafood mix), mixed bag of salad, and oil and vinegar dressing (a teaspoon of each).
- 115g (4oz) of chicken tikka pieces (ready made) with a cucumber, tomato and feta cheese salad, 10ml (2 tsp) of yoghurt and mint for the dressing.

## Dinner (choose one a day)

- Chicken kebabs (without skin) with stir-fried broccoli, mushrooms and peppers. Use soy sauce and ginger to flavour.
- Grilled steak, steamed spinach and mushrooms, and a side rocket salad with Parmesan cheese shavings.
- Oven-roasted vegetables (use at least seven different vegetables and drizzle a little olive oil on top), grilled fish with lemon and ginger and a mozzarella and tomato salad.
- Grilled chicken breast (without skin), with grilled vegetables and olive oil, and mashed cauliflower and carrots.
- Grilled salmon, spinach and raw carrots with low-fat yoghurt.
- Roasted sweet potato with two matchbox-sized portions of cheese, grilled courgettes, mushrooms and aubergine, and a side salad.
- 115g (4oz) grilled salmon, with stir-fried mangetout peas, baby corn, broccoli and carrots.

## Snacks (choose two a day)

- Four squares of dark chocolate (70 per cent cocoa solids).
- Fat-free yoghurt and sugar-free jelly.
- About 40g (1½oz) cheese of any type.

- Twenty to thirty olives or nuts.
- Low-fat fromage frais (small tub).
- Low-fat yoghurt (small tub).

### Drink options (daily)
- Tea or coffee.
- Diet colas.
- 2 litres (3½ pints) of water.
- 150ml (¼ pint) skimmed milk.
- Herbal teas.
- Tomato juice.

After two weeks you can add one of the following to breakfast, lunch or dinner each day:

- A jacket potato (without butter).
- Half a cup (raw measurement) of wholemeal pasta.
- Two slices of wholemeal bread.
- Half a cup (raw measurement) of brown rice.
- A piece of fruit, but not bananas.

## Smart party nibbles

By the time you've reached the end of this chapter you should fit perfectly into your party clothes, but just to make sure you don't sabotage your efforts with party food and drink bingeing, here's how to make some smarter and healthier food and drink swaps when you're out.

**tip**

How hungry are you? Work out the difference between being hungry and being bored or peckish. Next time you feel a craving for something, rate your hunger on a scale of one to ten. If you're not hitting seven you're not hungry.

### Drinks

**Instead of** a Breezer (alcopop), which clocks in at 200 calories a bottle, and 13g (about ½oz) of sugar,
**Choose** a glass of champagne, which has 95 calories and negligible sugar.

**Instead of** a creamy liqueur, which has 170 calories, 11g (about ¼oz) of sugar and 8g (just under ¼oz) of fat,
**Choose** Tia Maria, which has 150 calories and is fat-free.

**Instead of** a spirit with a high caffeine mixer (a rum and coke), which has around 170 calories, and 28g (1oz) of sugar, not to mention as much caffeine as a strong cup of coffee,
**Choose** a glass of red wine, which has 119 calories, negligible sugar and no caffeine.

**Instead of** a margarita cocktail, which has 160 calories and 7g (almost ¼oz) of sugar,
**Choose** a gin and slimline tonic, which has only 55 calories and no sugar.

**Instead of** a Sea Breeze (vodka, grapefruit and cranberry), which has 170 calories and 13g (almost ½oz) of sugar,
**Choose** half a pint of lager, which has only 118 calories and 8g (just under ¼oz) of sugar.

## Party bites

*Instead of* rich creamy cheeses, which have in excess of 10g (¼oz) of fat,
*Choose* goat's cheese, which just has 6g (less than ¼oz) of fat.

*Instead of* sour cream dips, which have around 10g (¼oz) of fat,
*Choose* salsa, which has 2–4g (less than ⅛oz) of fat and lots more goodness.

*Instead of* small crispy fries, which absorb lots of fat,
*Choose* potato wedges: the bigger the potatoes the less fat they absorb, meaning you could save up to 10g (¼oz) of fat.

*Instead of* fried chicken,
*Choose* baked chicken, and then take the skin off; it could save you 30g (1oz) of fat.

*Instead of* rich puddings, like trifle or fruit cakes, which can be loaded with around 300 calories a portion,
*Choose* a mince pie – it has a 100 calories less.

*Instead of* crisps, 30g (1oz) of which will give you around 170 calories,
*Choose* pretzels, which contain about 114 calories.

## Lazy party food choices

If there don't seem to be any obviously healthy choices (something to be aware of if you happen to be the hostess), here are the best protein-based (rather than fat- and carbo-hydrate-based) party nibbles that won't pile on the pounds:

- Mini-sausages (as long as they haven't been fried).
- Chicken (without skin).
- Sausages wrapped in bacon (but not pastry).
- Cold meats, such as turkey and ham.
- Cheeses, but leave the crackers alone.
- Dips with crudités, not bread.
- Smoked salmon.
- Chocolate (without a creamy centre).
- Olives.
- Nuts.

## Five ways to cut 100 calories

1. Drink fizzy water and lime at the pub instead of a glass of wine.
2. Swap your KitKat for an apple at 4.00 p.m.
3. Take the skin off your piece of chicken before you cook and eat it.
4. Don't spread butter or margarine on your toast, just have jam or honey.
5. Have a jacket potato instead of chips.

# The 'get-me-into-that-dress' exercise plan

### The hot 15 fitness rules

1. Follow the instructions and don't cheat.
2. Only work out for one hour at the most, four times a week.
3. Warm up and warm down for five minutes before exercising to help you avoid injury.
4. Always drink water throughout (or you'll pass out).
5. Eat at least one hour before your workout, for energy.
6. See a doctor before you start exercising if you have a lot of weight to lose, and/or you have an injury or are pregnant.
7. Don't overdo it – this is the number-one reason why people stop exercising.
8. Give yourself a day's break in between each workout for your body to recover.
9. Wear the right workout gear – especially on your feet.
10. Workout at the right intensity; you should feel breathless – not be able to sing along to MTV.
11. Build momentum by doing the exercises every other day; this way you'll force yourself to make the plan a habit.
12. Don't fool yourself; everyone has an hour in a day when they can workout (if not, get up half an hour earlier and go to bed half an hour later).

13. If you have no willpower, enlist a fit friend to be your exercise buddy.
14. Stick the dress you want to wear where you can see it every day as motivation.
15. Don't give up. Remind yourself it's only a one-month plan (12 to 16 days' worth of exercise in a month, to be precise).

## The cardiovascular bit

In order to lose weight you have to do some fat-burning exercise as well as toning. This means you have to get active four times a week for at least 20 minutes (active = breathless to the point that it's uncomfortable to talk as you workout. If you can sing along to MTV you're not moving fast enough). The options for a cardio workout are as follows. Pick one and increase the intensity each week, or try a different activity each week.

### 1 Fast walking/power walking

This is not just a gentle stroll round to the shops, but a powerful fast-walk that should occur in the following way:

1. Your heel strikes the ground first.
2. The foot rolls through, pushing you off the toes.
3. As you push off the toes, engage the muscles in your bottom (your glutes) and your upper leg and hamstring.
4. Swing your arms as you walk; this helps with balance and hip movement.

5. Your body should be upright at all times, with your stomach pulled in.
6. Stay in rhythm, and when you feel it's easy, increase your speed and choose inclines to challenge you even more.
7. Walk for 40 minutes, four times a week.

## 2 Cycling

Once again, the aim here is to get some exercise not to free-wheel down a hill.

1. Start off at a medium pace and cycle non-stop for 20–30 minutes, while pulling in your stomach muscles and not tensing your shoulders; focus on your leg muscles.
2. Week two: cycle at a very fast pace for one minute, then at a medium pace for three minutes to recover, and then repeat for 30 minutes.
3. Weeks three and four: lift your bottom off the seat (this will make you work harder), and cycle at a medium pace for 30 minutes; challenge yourself with inclines and hills.

## 3 Running

To run effectively, the most important fact to remember is always to move heel to toe (obvious but not many people do it):

1. As you take a step your heel should hit the ground first and your body weight should move through the foot into the toe.

2. Avoid looking down as you run. The average head weighs 4.5kg (10lb), so looking down pulls your body out of alignment and it will hurt your neck and shoulders. Focus instead in looking out in front of you.

3. Don't pound the ground. While running is a high-impact sport, you don't have to hit the ground with force (this can injure your knees). Again think upwards and release the tension in your upper body as you land.

4. Finally, when you run don't aim to bounce, or lift the feet too far off the ground and/or land on your toes. To run properly you should always land on your heels and use short, easy strides, not big bounding ones.

## tips

Relax as you run. Don't tense your upper body as you run. This makes it harder to breathe and will reduce your stamina. Hold yourself from your stomach (belly button to spine) also known as your core, not from your chest, and imagine your upper body being loose and relaxed.

## Week one

*Walk and run for 30 minutes*
Run for two minutes; walk for two minutes (repeat three times).

Briskly walk for four minutes, and then run for two minutes and repeat three times (18 minutes in total).

### Five ways to burn 100 calories

1. Make your bed every day: plump up your pillows, take off the sheets and turn your mattress over, and then remake your bed.
2. Run up the stairs and walk down for ten minutes.
3. Dance around your bedroom to your favourite CD for 15 minutes.
4. Walk to work for a change (or to your friend's house).
5. Do 30 minutes of yoga in your front room.

## Week two

*Walk and run for 30 minutes*
Run for three minutes, walk for two minutes and repeat three times (for 15 minutes). Then run for four minutes, walk for one minute and repeat three times (for 15 minutes).

## Week three

*Run and walk for 30 minutes*
Run for eight minutes, walk for two minutes and repeat three times.

## *Week four*

*Run*
Run for 30 minutes non-stop.

# The firming-up bit

## Essential equipment

### Dynaband

The Dynaband is a long piece of stretchy plastic rather like a long elastic band (and costs relatively little from any sports store – see Resources). Its key strength is that it works against your body's resistance and helps strengthen muscles to give definition and toning. Shorten the band to increase the resistance. The bands are colour coded – green for beginners, purple for those who exercise a lot and grey for the very strong.

### Swiss ball

A Swiss ball is a large inflatable ball also known as a stability ball or fitball. Because the ball is full of air, it has an unstable surface, so when you're sitting or lying on it and working major muscle groups, the smaller less-used muscles are also forced to work, to balance and stabilise the major muscles. You therefore get a more intense and powerful workout. The balls come in small, medium and large

sizes; you should opt for a medium size unless you're super tall. Make sure you buy a good quality ball that has been tested to high standards, so it won't pop when you bounce up and down on it. Also be sure to pump it up to the right volume; the ball shouldn't sink when you sit on it (see Resources).

## Week one

### Lunge

Works on your thighs, calves and bottom.

1. With both legs together, breathe in and take a big stride forwards with your right leg.
2. Drop down until your right thigh is parallel to the floor, and your right knee is bent to 90 degrees (keep your body upright, stomach pulled in and don't let your knee travel over your foot).
3. Breathe out and push up through both legs and step back to start position, and repeat.
4. Do two sets of ten repetitions on each leg.

### Step up

Works on your calves, thighs and hamstrings.

1. Place one leg on a step and keep the other on the floor.
2. Step up, lifting the back leg into the air in front of you and return to the start position. Use a slow and controlled movement to reap the best benefits.
3. Do two sets of ten repetitions on each leg.

### Squats

Works on your legs and bottom.

1. Stand with your feet hip-width apart and your knees slightly bent. Hold your arms out in front of you at shoulder height.
2. Breathe in and lower your body as if you were about to sit down in a chair (but keep your back straight and your stomach pulled in). Don't let your knees travel over your toes.
3. Breathe out and push through your heels to the start position.
4. Do two sets of 15 repetitions.

### Abdominal twist

Works on your waist and stomach.

1. Lie on your back with your knees bent, feet on the floor and hands behind your head (this is your start position).
2. Using your stomach muscles, lift your upper body off the ground and twist your left shoulder and elbow towards your right knee.
3. Return to the start position and repeat ten times, and then swap sides.
4. Do two sets of 12 repetitions.

### Press-ups

Works on your arms and stomach.

1. Kneel on all fours, and then move your knees back and lower your hips, so there is a straight line between your knees and

shoulders. Keep your hands directly under your shoulders (this is your start position).
2. Breathe out, bend your arms and lower your body towards the floor. Keeping the straight line (no curved back or high bottom).
3. Breathe in and press up to the start position.
4. Do two sets of ten repetitions.

### Dynaband bicep curl

Works on your arms.

1. Stand with your feet hip-width apart and stand on the Dynaband, grabbing hold of each end with your hands.
2. Keeping your arms by your sides, palms facing away from your body, pull the Dynaband upwards, squeezing your biceps (upper-arm muscles) as you pull. Keep the movement slow and controlled, and don't lift your shoulders as you pull.
3. Do two sets of 12 repetitions.

### Tricep dip

Works the flabby bits under your arms.

1. Sit on a chair and place your hands next to your thighs on the front edge of the chair.
2. Keeping your feet flat on the floor, slide your bottom off the chair so your weight is transferred to your arms (this is your start position).
3. Breathe in and lower your body to floor, then exhale and, using your arms, push your body up again.
4. Do two sets of 12 repetitions.

# Week two

### Step jumps
Works thighs, legs and bottom.

1. Place your right foot on a step and keep the left foot on the floor.
2. Using a fast jumping movement, swap legs over by changing legs mid-air.
3. Keep going for 30 seconds, take a 20 second rest and repeat three times.

### Hamstring curls on a Swiss ball
Works on your hamstrings.

1. Lie on the floor and place your legs on a Swiss ball.
2. Digging your heels into the ball, lift your pelvis off the floor (making sure your palms are facing upwards so the work is coming from your legs).
3. Keeping your pelvis up, pull the ball slowly in towards your bottom and roll it out again in a slow and steady movement.
4. Do three sets of 15 repetitions.

### Squats
(See week one.)

### *Press-ups on a Swiss ball*

Works on your triceps, chest and shoulders.

1. Kneel behind a Swiss ball, and then, lying on top of it, roll forwards, until your legs are stretched out and your arms are supporting you on the floor (your body should be in a straight line).
2. Now lower your chest to the floor and use your arms to push you back up (your legs shouldn't move).
3. Do three sets of eight repetitions.

### *Abdominal curl on a Swiss ball*

Works on your waist and stomach.

1. Lie back on a Swiss ball with your knees bent, and feet on the floor. Place your hands behind your head (this is your start position – if you feel wobbly don't worry, that's the whole point).
2. Using your stomach muscles, lift your upper body off the ball and twist your left shoulder and elbow towards your right side.
3. Return to the start position and repeat ten times. Then repeat but this time twist your right shoulder and elbow towards your left side.
4. Repeat the exercise twice.

### *Russian twist*

Works on your abdominal/stomach and lower back.

1. Lie on the floor and lift your legs to a 90-degree angle. Keeping your shoulders on the floor and your arms stretched out

(think: snow-angel position), roll your legs to the left and hold (don't let them fall to the ground).

2. Using your stomach, pull your legs back to centre and roll them over to the right, and repeat.

3. Do two sets of 12 repetitions.

### Dynaband lateral raises

Works on your shoulders.

1. Keeping your feet hip-width apart, place the Dynaband under both feet and take hold of each end of the band.

2. Slowly raise your arms out to the side to shoulder height and then return to the start position. Use a slow and controlled movement.

3. Do two sets of 12 repetitions.

### Dynaband bicep curl

(See week one, but this time wrap each end of the band more tightly around each hand to increase the resistance and to make the exercise harder.)

## Week three

### Static lunge with Dynaband curl

Works on your biceps, bottom, thighs and hamstrings.

1. Take a large step forwards and place your right foot in front of you. Place the Dynaband under the right leg and take hold of each end.

2. Now drop down (as in a normal lunge) but curl your arms upwards as you lower.
3. Straighten arms as you rise up again.
4. Do three sets of 15 repetitions.

### Squat with lateral raises with a Dynaband

Works on your shoulders, bottom, thighs and hamstrings.

1. Stand with your feet hip-width apart and place the Dynaband under your feet and grab both ends in your hands.
2. Breathe in and lower your body as if you were about to sit down in a chair, but as you lower, bring your arms out to your sides to shoulder height.
3. Lower as you come back to the start position, and repeat.
4. Do three sets of 15 repetitions.

### Abdominal curl on a Swiss ball

(See week two. Do two sets of 15 repetitions.)

### Glute extension with a Dynaband

Works on your bottom and lower back.

1. Tie the Dynaband around a pole or banister (so that it's looped around the pole/banister).
2. Facing the pole, step into the loop with one leg. Now lean forwards and hold the pole, and then take a step back so there is tension in the band (this is your start position).
3. Now, pull the leg inside the loop as far back as it can go with

the leg remaining straight at all times and return to the start position. Swap legs.

4. Do two sets of 15 repetitions on each leg.

### Inner thigh workout with a Dynaband

Works on your inner and outer thighs.

1. Tie the band around a pole and step into the loop with one leg, turn sideways and then pull the band so that it's relatively tight. Place your hands on your hips.
2. Keeping the leg in the loop straight, pull the leg across your other leg, and repeat. Swap legs.
3. Do two sets of 15 repetitions on each leg.

### Press-ups (three sets of ten repetitions)

(See week one, but this time do a full press-up not one on your knees.)

# Week four: circuit

Do 30 seconds of each exercise and then take a 15 second rest and repeat each exercise three times.

### Static lunge with lateral raises

Works on your shoulders, thighs and legs.

1. Take a large step forwards and place your right foot in front of you. Place the Dynaband under the right leg and take hold of each end of the band.

2. Now drop down (as in a normal lunge) but at the same time raise your arms out to the side to shoulder height.
3. Lower as you straighten, and repeat.

### Swiss ball press-up and tuck

Works on your triceps, chest, shoulders and stomach.

1. Kneel behind a Swiss ball and then lie on top of it. Roll forwards, until your legs are stretched out and your arms are supporting you on the floor (this is your start position).
2. Lower your chest to floor and, as you use your arms to push you back up, curl the legs in towards your chest. Return to the start position, and repeat.

### Step jumps

(See week two.)

### Swiss ball abdominal curls (one leg raised)

Works on your waist and stomach.

1. Lie back on a Swiss ball with your knees bent and feet on the floor. Place your hands behind your head and lift your right leg off the floor (if you feel wobbly don't worry, that's the whole point).
2. Now, using your stomach muscles, lift your upper body off the ball and twist your left shoulder and elbow towards your right leg. Return to the start position and repeat.

### Squat with shoulder press, with Dynaband

Works on your shoulders, bottom, thighs and hamstrings.

1. Stand with your feet hip-width apart and place the Dynaband under your feet. Grab both ends in your hands and hold your hands either in front of you or to the sides at shoulder height (palms facing forwards).
2. Breathe in and lower your body as if you were about to sit down in a chair. As you lower, push your arms upwards and then return them to shoulder height as you straighten up. Return to the start position and repeat.

### Russian twist

(See week two.)

### Glute extension with a Dynaband

(See week three.)

### Inner thigh workout with a Dynaband

(See week three.)

## The high-heel workout

It takes balance, good posture, strong stomach muscles and practice to dance the night away in a pair of three-inch heels. Here's how to get your legs in party shape so that it's not a case of murder on the dance floor.

Do all the following exercises three times a week for toned and honed legs.

### *Wide squat*

A squat is the perfect exercise for shaping your inner thighs, and toning your bottom, and the front and back of your thighs.

1. Stand with your feet wide apart and your toes turned out. Keeping your hands on your hips, lower your bottom towards the floor, keeping your upper body upright (pull that tummy in).
2. Go as low as you can go without wobbling forwards, and then push back through your feet and contract your bottom to the start position.
3. Do three sets of 15 repetitions.

### *Stand on one leg*

This works the muscles around your ankles and the ligaments in your leg, which are essential if you want to walk across a room in heels without stumbling.

1. Pull your stomach in, take a deep breath and lift your right leg up, bending your knee.
2. Hold for a count of ten. If you wobble, lift your arms out to the side to keep your balance. Swap legs.
3. Repeat ten times on each leg.

### Toe lifts

This helps stop your toes cramping up and your feet hurting when balanced on stiletto points.

1. Stand up with your feet hip-width apart (your hips are smaller than you think so don't stand too wide).
2. Press your heels into the floor and then try to lift up your toes and the front of the foot leaving the ball of the foot on the floor.
3. One foot at a time, repeat ten times.

### Leg circles

Gives your legs a lovely all-over lean look.

1. Lie on your back on the floor, and pull your belly button to your spine to keep your back supported.
2. Bend one knee and leave the foot firmly on the ground. Lift the other leg about 13–20cm (5–8in) off the ground and point the foot.
3. Keeping your tailbone and hips firmly on the ground, make five small circles clockwise and another five anticlockwise, and then change legs. Make sure the movement starts from the tops of your thighs (imagine your whole leg rotating).
4. Do three sets of 12 repetitions.

### Inner thigh squeeze

Stops inner-thigh chafing and bottom sagging.

1. Lie on your back with your legs bent and your feet on the floor.
2. Place a relatively hard cushion between your knees and hold it there. Take a deep breath and, as you exhale, lift your hips off the ground and squeeze the cushion with your thighs for eight counts.
3. Keeping your hips up, repeat the move ten times.

### Side lifts

This tones your outer thighs and whittles down your waist.

1. Lie on your left side, with your knees slightly bent towards your chest and your head resting on your left arm.
2. Raise your right leg and stretch it out, pushing through the heel. In this position lift it 7.5cm (3in) (pull your tummy in), imagining your leg being pulled straight at all times. Repeat 15 times.
3. Turn over and swap legs.
4. Do three sets of 15 repetitions.

### Static lunge

This is the best leg exercise for fat burning and muscle definition.

1. Take a large step forward and place one foot in front of you (keep your hips pointing forwards and your tummy pulled in).
2. Now, bend your knees so your front leg drops forwards (don't let your knee travel over your toes) and your back leg drops

down. Push back through the heel of your foot to rise (this will work your bottom), and repeat with the other leg.

3. Do two sets of 20 repetitions.

### Plié with press back

This will give you ballet-dancer posture in your heels.

1. Stand with your feet turned out at 45 degrees, and slightly wider than shoulder-width apart.
2. Keep your knees soft (not locked straight) and bend your legs, until your thighs are parallel to the floor. Raise your arms to chest height as you bend for balance.
3. In this position pulse (push) your inner thighs in and out four times and then squeeze your bottom while you return to standing.
4. Do two sets of 15 repetitions.

### Beats and paddles

For a perfectly toned bottom.

1. Lie face down on the floor, pulling in your stomach muscles and pushing your pubic bone to the floor.
2. Lift your legs off the ground about 5cm (2in) and pulse your legs and heels together for a count of 50.
3. Relax, then go back into position and beat your feet up and down in a small movement, as if you were paddling, for 50 counts.

## *Party hard and stay fit*

The good news about being a party diva is that you can combine staying fit with having a good time as long as you can drag yourself away from the buffet table and hit the dance floor. Apart from the obvious aerobic benefits to your heart and lungs, dancing helps increase muscle strength, promote flexibility and improve alignment and balance. The fat-burning quota is also higher than most people think, with the average person burning around three to ten calories a minute. This means that a medium-paced salsa class could work off around 350 to 400 calories an hour – or basically your entire lunch!

If gym stuff and going for a run is not your thing, here are the classes to sign up for pre-party.

### *Ballroom*

We're talking the waltz, the tango and the quickstep, but far from being the domain of the blue-rinsed brigade, ball-room has shed its stuffy and dull image. Do it right and you will strengthen your abdominal area, legs and lower back (as well as look good on the dance floor at weddings).

### *Belly dancing*

The hot dance favourite of the moment. Do it right and you'll realise that there are parts of your body (especially the stomach and legs) that you haven't moved in years.

### Line dancing

This is one of the most popular dance classes in the UK, with studies showing it has been tried by one in 25 people. It's not the most aerobic class you'll ever do, but it's fantastic for the legs, bottom and stomach.

### Ballet

The New York City Ballet classes found at most gyms and on DVD combine elements of ballet with an emphasis on muscle conditioning, alignment, balance and flexibility. Do it regularly and devotees say it can give you a longer, leaner body profile and better posture.

### Salsa

This is a fast-paced dance class performed in couples. It's the most cardiovascular of dance classes, meaning your heart, legs, stomach and arms will all get a fantastic workout. Salsa is particularly frenzied and takes concentration and co-ordination, so if you fancy a slower, sexier class try merengue or the lambada.

### Swing/jive/ceroc

This is about as rock 'n' roll as you can get in a dance class and, therefore, classes are highly aerobic as well as fun. Get to grips with the high-impact moves and you're guaranteed toned legs, buttocks and increased stamina and mobility.

## *Burn the calories the party way*

OK, we know you're super-lazy and may not want to do any of the above. If so, the good news is you can still burn ample energy/calories on the day of your party by doing all of the following:

|  | Calories |
| --- | --- |
| Domestic-goddess duties | 150 |
| Moving furniture | 150 |
| Cooking all day | 160 |
| Shopping for food/decorations | 280 |
| Running down stairs to answer door | 300 |
| Decorating a room | 200 |
| Dancing (non-energetic) | 200 |
| Dancing (energetically) | 400 |

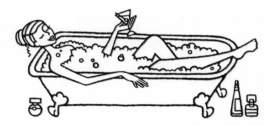

# 20 ways
## to get into that party dress

### 1 Pat your pizza

You've seen it on the US sitcoms and now do it yourself. Blotting a piece of pizza with a sheet of kitchen roll can eliminate approximately 14 per cent of the total fat and 17 per cent of the saturated fat according to the Health Smart Institute in Florida.

### 2 Stand up straight

Believe it or not, posture is everything. Standing up straight not only evenly distributes your weight, but can also allow you to actually get into that dress you were slouched over five minutes ago and, better still, look great in it.

### 3 Workout through lunch

Not only will you eat less at the end of it, but also studies from the University of Texas show you'll be faster, stronger and more flexible if you workout at lunchtime rather than earlier in the day.

### 4 Hold it until you shake

During a workout when your muscles start to quiver like jelly, they're fatigued. Meaning, the longer you hold a pose the more you increase your strength and endurance.

### 5 Use challenging weights

If you're at the gym, as tempting as it is to lift girlie weights for show, heaving something altogether more challenging is essential if your aim is to make your body give up its fat for muscle. This means choose a weight that takes effort (but not pain) to lift.

### 6 Eat less, but more times a day

Five small meals a day is the best diet tip, as it keeps your blood sugar level raised all day and stops chocolate cravings. Plus, a huge meal will only deplete your energy and make you feel so sluggish that you'll be heading for a snooze, and so won't burn off an ounce.

**7 Tighten your bum**
Clench your buttocks and hold for a count of ten, then release and repeat ten times. Do this on the way to and from work, and whenever you're in a queue and you'll have a pert peach of a bottom in no time.

**8 Cut out all salt**
Salt makes you retain fluid and could make your dress ultra tight even once you've toned and trimmed yourself. Cutting your intake in half by eating fresh and not processed foods will minimise the bloat and could help you to lose an extra 1.3kg (3lb).

**9 Rethink your drink**
Fizzy colas and artificial sweeteners can cause your belly to swell and bloat. Drink a tall glass of still water flavoured with lemon to keep the belly look at bay.

**10 Speed it up**
Make every moment count when you're exercising. Always work at a level seven or eight (in terms of how difficult you find it to keep going). You'll burn the same amount of calories in a 20-minute fast-paced walk, as you would in a 40-minute slower one.

**11 Eat before you sweat**
Morning exercise and breakfast are the keys to kick-starting your metabolic rate and burning calories all day. Eat something high in carbohydrates an hour before you start exercising to help you work harder. Opt for a banana or toast.

**12 Don't fixate on when you eat, but what you eat**
It's a huge misconception that food eaten late at night turns to fat more quickly than food eaten before 6.00 p.m. because it's not being burned off. The truth is it's what your total calorie intake is for the day that determines fat stores.

**13 Swimming is not the best all-round exercise**
Not when it comes to weight loss, because most people don't swim fast enough or for long enough. If you've only

got 30 minutes you're better off going for a run, as it will help you to burn 140 calories more.

**14** **Think portions**
Eating healthily but not losing weight? It could be a question of portion size not food that's holding you back. Portions equal a handful, a small cup or a piece of meat the size of your palm.

**15** **Eat less than your boyfriend**
Men have a higher calorie intake a day than women simply because they are bigger and need more fuel. If you match your boyfriend plate for plate, you're asking for excess poundage and you'll gain it faster than him simply because women already naturally have more body fat than men.

**16** **Don't skip breakfast**
Studies show that many overweight people skip the first meal of the day because they think it saves them calories, when in fact all it does is drop the body's blood sugar level resulting in

powerful hunger cravings and a higher calorie intake at lunchtime.

**17** **Be positive, but realistic**
If you're 1.6m/5ft 5in and weigh around 68kg/10st 10lb you're not going to look like a teeny-tiny pop star in your party dress. However, this doesn't mean you won't look and feel fantastic as long as you aren't bombarding yourself with unrealistic expectations.

**18** **Don't drink your calories**
So, you're at the gym three times a week, you've cut out junk food and chocolate and still your dress feels tight. If so, you could be drinking your calories. Just one glass of wine a night can add between 100–200 calories (that's a whopping 1,400 extra calories and 225g (½lb) of fat a week) and sabotage your best efforts.

**19** **Don't lie to yourself**
If you feel and say you don't eat much and yet everything feels tight, you need to pay more attention to your diet.

Start by noting down every piece of food you eat (and, yes, nibbling counts). Keep a food diary for a week to keep yourself in check.

## 20 Ignore celebrity diets

If you're a diet bore (that is, you can recite the calories of more than three foods and you've been on every diet going) it's time to STOP. The key to weight loss is simple – eat less and do more. Eat all the things that you know are healthy, get moving more often and you'll be able to get into any dress you want, any time.

# chapter 4

# How to flirt

All of us have suffered pangs of pre-party anxiety ranging from 'What if no-one speaks to me?' to 'What will I say if the guy I fancy speaks to me?' and 'What will I do if my ex appears with a gorgeous new girlfriend on his arm?' Apart from running screaming from the room, the solution is to bolster yourself with ample amounts of pre-party confidence before you even step into the brink.

Confidence at a party has a number of pluses going for it. Apart from being an effective anti-embarrassment tool (if you feel confident you're less likely to get drunk and end up dancing on a table-top with your knickers on your head), it will boost your sex appeal and help you to break the ice with the less confident. Better still, it will make you the kind of guest people fight over. Meaning, lots more party invitations for you.

*tip*

Everyone's as anxious as you. Don't imagine everyone else is having a better time than you are. The truth is they are just as worried about meeting new people, being entertaining and looking good.

However, the simple truth is, most of us find it hard to be a social butterfly, the kind of person who flits glamorously from group to group while being wildly funny and intelligent all night. The reality is if you're like the average party-goer, you're probably someone who can muster a few witty comments with people you know, dance a bit with someone you like and maybe even talk to one or two people you've never set eyes on before. Which is all fine and well if you have a good time, but to double your enjoyment factor it pays to know how to spread your social wings; if not to become a guest in a million then at least to have an outrageously fabulous time that you'll still be talking about months later.

# The lazy guide to schmoozing

## Step one: get the event into perspective

Job interviews are daunting, public speaking events are nerve-wracking, and first dates are guaranteed to turn you into a quivering plate of jelly, but parties are not nightmarish events. If you feel they are, you need to get the event into perspective and remind yourself that this is an invitation to have a good time not to commit social suicide. And a good time means not backing out because you think you look too fat in your dress, or because you're afraid of what to say, and/or because you don't know anyone but the hostess. If someone has bothered to invite you it means that:

- They want you to be there.
- They like you.
- They think you'll have a good time.
- They expect you to come (unless you say otherwise).
- They think you'll get on with the other guests.

So, as a guest your objective should be simply to enjoy yourself, feel great and not worry about what everyone else is thinking about you (clue: they are too busy thinking about themselves to worry about what you're wearing).

## *Step two: make an entrance*

When it comes to parties always start as you mean to go on. Meaning, don't enter a party as if you're ashamed about arriving alone; in other words, don't skulk about, looking for a familiar face to cling on to and waiting until three cocktails boost your confidence and/or a group of real friends turn up. If this sounds familiar (or you're someone who is regularly found in the kitchen at parties or behind the yucca), then it's worth knowing how to master making an entrance. Whether it's into a room, into a conversation or into someone's life – it can change your party fortunes for the better.

To get it right:

- Always hold your head up high as you walk in so that people will notice you, and stand briefly in the doorway (mainly for effect).
- Smile – a good honest smile (rather than a showbiz grimace). The best way to do this is to imagine a funny event from the past and then let a natural smile come to your face and hold it there.
- Look at people and say 'Hello' as you walk past even if you don't know them. Remember it's about showing you're a friendly person worth getting to know.
- Let your host do the work: let him or her introduce you to other people. Good hosts will find you someone that you have at least one thing in common with before abandoning you to conversational doom.
- Head for the drinks table especially if nerves get the better of you, as you are always guaranteed to find people to talk to there and you can make small talk about beer and whether red wine is better than white etc.

### Step three: consider your party aims

While you're getting a sense of space and who's who, now is a good time to consider your party aims. If your plan is to get so drunk you can't stand, your next move is pretty obvious. If, however, you want to meet someone new, catch someone's eye and generally have a good time, take a long hard look around you and consider the following:

- Where is the best position in the room to catch someone's eye?
- Who is the best person to help you reap maximum party fun?
- Who you should avoid?
- Where is the toilet, in case you need to make a quick escape from someone?

## Step four: work out who's at the heart of the party

If you can spot the group that is the life and soul of the party you should hot foot it over there and make contact. This is because this is where the party action will be. These people will not only know who's who, but also who's single and who's not, how to grab someone's attention and where the secret drinks stash is hidden. Good news for you because they are a shortcut to working a party. To get their attention:

- Strike up a conversation that either establishes instant intimacy or instant confidence. This means either flatter their dresses, shoes or hair or make them laugh.
- Don't say, 'Isn't this party rubbish?' (the chances are they'll be either the host or dating him) or 'I just broke up with my boy-friend and I don't know anyone' (it sounds as desperate as it is).
- Don't focus on just one person in a group but pull in two so you won't get stuck if they prove to be party poopers in disguise.

## Step five: fake it to make it

Everyone fakes the schmoozing to some degree. Whether it's by donning an outfit that instils her with sex goddess-like status, or by losing herself with the help of a few drinks. However, you can't get away without making conversation for the whole of a party, no matter how sexy you look. Which is why when you're faking the schmoozing it's important not to get too dark and heavy. People do not come to parties to discuss the realities of the Third World debt. They come to be silly, have a laugh and have a good time. Don't be the person who brings in the doom, but:

- Do lie outrageously to make people laugh.
- Do exit gracefully if someone looks bored.
- Do keep moving round the room, as this way you'll schmooze your way in with a variety of groups, not just one.

## Step six: don't land yourself with a dud group

While it can be comforting to head for the group you feel most comfortable with, say the couples in a corner or the singletons in the kitchen, or even the music lovers huddled round the CDs, don't be so quick to ask for membership. Certain groups do not make for good party fun especially if they have no intention of mixing and mingling and only want to talk the same old, same old …

Place yourself slightly out of your comfort zone and I guarantee you'll have more fun.

---

## Party guests to avoid

- The singletons lamenting where all the good men are.
- The beer drinkers swigging straight from the keg.
- The couples talking babies and mortgages.
- The two best friends, who don't really want you to join them.
- The femme fatale who will end up elbowing you in the eye to get to a man.
- The man who's just broken up with his girlfriend.
- The person who sways perilously as you talk to them.
- The man who talks to your breasts.

---

# Flirting

Of course, there's more to parties than letting your hair down and dancing the night away. If you're single and on the prowl, the chances are you'll want to flex those flirting muscles and have a go at pulling in someone you like. If you can flirt with your eyes and use your body to its best advantage, and know what to say when you like someone, you can skip this section. However, if you're more likely to turn to stone when a good-looking man comes over, here's all you'll ever need to know about flirting.

## *The power of flirting*

Contrary to popular opinion the best flirts in the world are not the prettiest, smartest and thinnest girls but the people who know how to make the most out of their verbal and more importantly non-verbal signals. These are the ideal lazy girls – women who can work a room without moving and pull a man without going in for a major overkill. The good news is this could be you, but before we start with that, here's a few ways not to flirt:

### *Don't rely on alcohol*

Studies show 80 per cent of people drink for courage when trying to grab someone's attention. Sadly this is bad news because alcohol also lowers your inhibitions meaning you're more likely to say the wrong thing, make a fool of yourself and go further than you would when you're sober.

### *Don't hold on to someone for dear life*

If you're flirting with someone who wants you to flirt with him you won't have to attach yourself to his ankle to get him to stick around. If you do have to hold on with white knuckles you're on to a loser.

### Don't oversell yourself

It's tempting to give a man your whole CV and complete run down of Brownie badges, but it's also horribly off-putting to have to stand and listen to someone do the big sell – so don't!

### Don't interrogate him

Likewise, don't rattle off a list of questions as long as your arm to someone you're trying to impress. He'll feel as if he's in a job interview and you'll end up feeling he hasn't asked anything about you.

### Be careful who you flirt with

Don't flirt with the host's boyfriend, your best friend's dad, and every single man you meet. Not only is this potentially embarrassing but also a recipe for disaster. For best results stick to single guys in your age range.

### Don't be self-absorbed

If you're too busy worrying what he thinks of you, or what your bottom looks like, you won't be able to flirt properly. To be an effective flirt you need to be outward not inward thinking.

### Don't be negative

The biggest turn off is to hear someone endlessly say negative things about themselves, their friends and their life. If you're a constant complainer, the message you're giving out is that it takes a lot to please you and you're hard work.

### Don't be overly familiar

We all have space issues. Some people like others to get up close and personal, while others would prefer you to keep your distance. If someone you're talking to is practically backed into a corner or has their hands out in front of them, you're getting too close and familiar for their liking – take a step back.

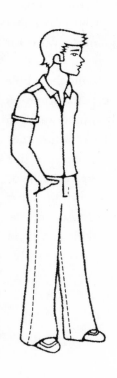

## How men see and hear your flirting signals:

- 55 per cent of messages come from your body language.
- 38 per cent come from the way your voice sounds – think tone, depth of voice and attitude.
- Only 7 per cent comes from what you're actually saying.

## How to flirt

When it comes to flirting, humour and good self-esteem will get you further than perfect make-up and a low-cut dress, simply because flirting is all about being charming. Also, as strange as this sounds, being a successful flirt is like being successful at anything – you need confidence: the ability to take measured risks and a degree of positivity to get to your goal. Meaning, if you start flirting thinking you're going to fail, or throw yourself at any man that moves, or flirt half-heartedly, it's not going to work for you.

If you're already feeling a bit wobbly about the whole thing, don't despair; before you hit the party scene go somewhere like a coffee shop and simply couple-watch to see how people interact with each other. Look for how they make contact, deal with space issues and generally flirt with their bodies. The aim here is not to copy other people's moves but instead to pick some helpful flirt hints that you can make your own. Next, practise, practise, practise with everyone you meet (within reason). This is a good way to get the flirt bug and generally feel more comfortable about flirting in a party situation.

Good practice flirt venues for pre-party experience include:

- Coffee shops
- Bookshops
- The gym
- Cinema queues
- Supermarkets
- Banks and post offices

Good people to practise your flirting on:

**The postman.** Aim: can you flirt when you're not looking your best?

**Shop assistants.** Aim: can you make a surly assistant do something for you without grumbling?

**Waiters.** Aim: can you make a waiter smile as he serves you a cappuccino?

**Taxi drivers:** Aim: can you find out something personal about them?

**Call-centre operators.** Aim: can you flirt on the phone?

**Men you work with (who you don't fancy).** Aim: can you attract their attention in a different way?

## Get noticed

To get noticed in a party situation all you have to do is know how to stand out in a crowd in a GOOD way. Of course people will notice you if you dance naked on a table, fall on your face, and tuck your skirt into your knickers, but the key is to get noticed in an 'Oh-my-god-who-is-she?' way. To do this, start by hanging around with people who look as if they are having a good time.

A study from the US discovered that people found it was hard to ignore and walk away from very sociable people. So, to grab any man's attention, smile, have a laugh and

*tip*

Find yourself a master flirt. And watch her moves. Successful flirts will show you that there's more to grabbing someone's attention then simply flicking your hair and staring. Watch to see how they work a room, get noticed and attract attention.

generally don't stand around trying to catch your reflection in your glass. Having said that, be sure not to stay attached to the group all night long and laugh at the top of your voice. Not only is this off-putting, but you also need to give a man adequate opportunity to get near you, without having to face you in front of all your friends.

## Mark your territory

Not literally, but let him know where you are in the room by making sure you're not everywhere at once. Remember you're no longer schmoozing. This means staying put in a particular area, so that he can muster up the courage to come over. Whizz from spot to spot and he'll either assume you're too busy for him or that you've left to go somewhere else. Good areas to loiter are: by the drinks, near the kitchen or simply a place that he can easily pretend he was just walking past.

## Don't be afraid to take risks

Successful flirts take risks. Wait for someone else to make the first move, and you could be waiting all your life. If you find taking a risk horribly difficult, it's time to look at your belief system. Do you believe nice girls don't do the asking? Are you convinced that if a man really liked you he'd come over? If so, that could be why you're single.

The simple fact is, flirting is about risk taking: the risk of being rejected, the risk of talking to a stranger you like the look of, and the risk of it all working out. If you're unable to take the plunge then you're basically closing the door on your inner flirt and sabotaging yourself before you even begin. Of course, the fear of rejection is a tough one, but if you never try, nothing will ever happen.

An easy way to start flirting is to take a calculated risk, that is, opt for someone you can sense likes you. Good clues that someone is interested include eye contact, smiling and body language. Look out for someone who is making excuses to get near you, someone who keeps looking at you and then glancing away, and someone who smiles a lot in your direction. Of course, these aren't guarantees that this is Mr Right but it's a good beginning.

## *Give clear signals*

It may be plain obvious to you and your friends, that (a) you fancy him; and (b) you're dropping huge flirt bombs, but the truth is many men are just useless at picking up signals. If you've been sending out hot come-hither looks and he's still looking but doing nothing, it's time to rev up your flirting. Firstly, don't assume he's not interested because he hasn't made it over. Men who are not interested will not look at you or keep glancing in your direction. Secondly, don't be too subtle with your flirting because this will confuse him. The lazy way to flirt is essentially to be clear and honest about what you're doing.

# tips

All the experts agree on one thing: the perfect tip for letting someone know you like them without feeling rejected if they decide they don't is to look at someone until they look at you, hold their gaze for under a second and then look away. Remember to look back and you'll have their attention if they like you.

The important flirt facts to remember are:

- Don't stare at a person – this is freaky and somewhat scary, and he'll notice you for the wrong reasons.
- Don't keep glancing nervously at him; he'll think there's something wrong.
- Do smile naturally so that he registers you as friendly rather than manic.
- Do keep looking until he gets the message or you get the message (clue: he'll look away and won't look back if he's not interested).

## Give him easy access

The next tip is to put yourself somewhere where he can walk over to you easily and start talking. Either hover by the drinks table, loiter by the CDs or start looking at something that might draw him over (a picture, books, out of a window), and then, when he does, start a normal conversation.

The key is to keep your conversation lively. Talking too slowly, pausing too long and taking too long to make your point is not only tedious for the other person but also it doesn't build what's known as rapport.

## *Build rapport*

Rapport is an essential ingredient of flirting because it gives you a non-verbal connection with the person you're speaking to, making them feel attached to you even if all you're doing is discussing the paintwork. To build rapport it's important to:

- Try to match the person's voice patterns. This means keeping an even tempo with them. Either talking just above their pace or below.
- Not be in love with the sound of your own voice. You should speak for roughly the same amount of time as the other person unless you want the other person to get bored with you.
- Notice his signals. Remember you can have the best flirting tools in the world but if you don't know how to read his signals you'll still be a hopeless flirt. 'I like you' signals are: moving closer to you, nodding and accidental-on-purpose touching; not-interested signals are: looking around while you are speaking, keeping a distance from you and calling you someone else's name!

## Think body language

Don't believe all you read about body language. It's not that easy to tell if someone's lying to you by the way their eyes turn, and having arms crossed against your chest isn't always a defensive stance. Having said that, body language is a powerful tool, and a technique known as 'mirroring' – repeating someone's words, body language and gestures – works because it subtly tells the person you're on their wavelength. However, always be careful not to copy a person's every move too obviously or say the same things, as that screams weird!

Mirror musts:

- Try to adopt the same volume and speed of speech that he's using.
- Use similar phrases that he's used.
- Sit in a similar fashion to him, that is, lean in when he does, sit back when he does.
- Every now and then use his name in a sentence.

### He likes you when:

- He moves closer every time you speak.
- He asks you questions about yourself.
- He accidentally finds ways to brush against you.

## Be careful what you say

As tempting as it is to spill all your beans at once, it pays when you're flirting to leave him guessing. No guy needs to know the name of your cat, what you ate for dinner and how you're just 'desperate' for a boyfriend. Mystery is 100 times more intriguing and enticing.

At the same time don't fish for compliments by putting yourself down all the time. Say you're fat enough times and the person you're talking too will start to believe you. To get a positive response be positive (notice how men never put themselves down).

How to be positive:

- Give out compliments; honest flattery is very flirtatious.
- Talk about your good traits – it's not boasting to say you're good at something.

## Be tactile

Touch him to show that you like him, but be careful what you do. Faces are off limits to people who don't know each other very well, as are the obvious bodily areas. But touching someone on the arm as you speak, playfully pushing their arm (gently) as you joke and if you're daring, touching their knee, all says I fancy you.

Kissing is also good flirtatious behaviour if you want to reel him in. However, we're not talking going for a full-on

French kiss but a gentle 'Hello there' kiss, which says, 'OK then, what next?'

And while I'm at it, it's always worth remembering that being sexually suggestive is not the same as flirting. While there is a sexual undertone to flirting, being OTT about sex or implying you're wild in bed only implies you want more from him ASAP and suggests that's all you want from him.

## *How to have a flirty conversation*

You can get all the body language and attraction signals right, but if you can't hold a flirty conversation then you're likely to blow all your hard work. To flirt successfully you have to be careful not to rush to fill all the silences with what's known as 'filler speak', that is, conversation that doesn't say very much at all or says too much.

The key to doing this is always to take a breath after someone speaks before you answer. This way you can consider what they have said, and give a response that doesn't sound panicked.

If you feel yourself being distracted by fears that he doesn't like you, refocus on the conversation by concentrating on each word he says. A good way to do this is to put pictures to his sentences, which not only helps you remember what he's saying but also gives you ideas for what to say next.

Next, be careful not to fire questions and talk over people, as this screams self-obsessed. Above all don't be afraid to show him your sexy side. This way you won't fall into the potential laddette/friend category, but as potential girl-friend material.

## *Notice when they fancy you*

Men who are interested act interested. They don't look around the room when you're speaking, yawn when you ask them something and generally make you work hard to keep their attention. This means, walk away if you're not getting the desired response and find someone who is will-ing to be flirted with. Another pointer to watch out for is men who like you will draw attention to themselves. They'll laugh loudly at your jokes, move in closer when you speak and will also be more tactile. Hidden 'I like you' moves include: touching your arm as you speak, looking at your mouth as you speak, and playing with their hair (bizarre but true).

If they guide you by your elbow or the small of your back, you're there and all your hard work has paid off!

# 20 ways
## to flirt successfully

**1 Choose the right outfit**
If you try too hard or wear something that isn't you, you're going to give off desperate vibes or spend the whole night trying to yank your skirt down. The style experts say always go for cleavage or legs, never both, and always leave something to the imagination.

**2 Act normal**
Also known as retain your dignity. In your pursuit to be noticed it can be tempting to gyrate and dance like a pole dancer on centre stage. This is great if that's your career but not so hot if you're trying to make an impression that counts.

**3 Relax**
It is a party and flirting is supposed to be fun. If you're on the verge of mania or tears, then something is going wrong with your flirting technique. If you feel yourself spiralling out of control, breathe out, smile and then start again.

**4 Don't play games**
Men are simple creatures; they don't understand the 'I fancy him so I'll ignore him' technique or the 'I fancy him so I'll talk to his friends' angle. If you just start chatting they'll naturally assume you fancy them because you've made the effort.

**5 Perfect your glance**
I've said it before and I'll say it again – to rope someone in, simply glance in their direction and look them in the eye. If you sneakily steal glances when they're not looking they'll just assume you don't want to be bothered.

**6 Don't wait to be asked**
Do a straw poll in your office right now and ask how many men like to be chatted up. The chances are it's the number one all-time flirt winner. Why? Well, simply because men get bored with having to put themselves on the line

constantly. Meaning, if you get in there first they'll not only be grateful but eager to flirt back.

## 7 Be sneaky

This is different from playing games because it's all about reeling a man in. This means getting him somewhere quiet away from his friends and into a private space. A good way to do this is feign deafness and suggest you go into the garden/kitchen/broom cupboard. If you're getting good radar signals from him, take him by the elbow and lead him to your quiet spot.

## 8 Touch him more

As human beings we all love to be touched, so try a subtle caress of the hand, an accidental brush against his leg and a squeeze of the arm as you're speaking – it will say and do wonders for him.

## 9 Avoid thinking too much

It's the kiss of death to flirting. 'Enjoy – don't worry' is the mantra to repeat to yourself if your mind starts wandering and worrying that your bum looks too big or that his eyes have glazed over.

## 10 Be unpredictable

That's inventive, not scary. Saying, 'So I'm told I'm a dead ringer for X [choose someone you're obviously not a dead ringer for to get a laugh]. What do you think?' is a good way to gauge humour levels and break the ice. Telling him he has cute feet might also work. Explaining why your mum and dad called you X won't grab his attention.

## 11 Don't be over-confident

Confidence counts but not if you're facing someone who is shy and/or apprehensive about why you've zeroed in on him. This doesn't mean squashing your natural exuberance but simply reining it in a bit, so that your laugh doesn't have him running for the door.

## 12 Don't flick your hair

Also known as don't let nerves take control of you. In a stressful situation it can be tempting to fidget, and while a certain amount of licking of lips and tossing of hair is fine, swinging your head about and letting your tics get the better of you, will kill the flirt moment. If you're feeling jittery, simply breathe and smile – it will cover a multitude of nerves.

## 13 Feel free to tease him

You don't have to be a doting, pathetic female to get the right reaction from a man – in fact most men liked to be teased in a good-natured way. Tips here include not to get too personal (no trading of insults about body parts and clothes) but simply to not be afraid to disagree.

## 14 Be fun to be with

This sounds obvious, but if your idea of a good conversation is to let rip with a litany of everything that's wrong with the party, men, your life and the music, you'll soon be left talking to yourself.

## 15 Ask open-ended questions

You may be a dab hand at conversation but you may have picked someone who isn't, so if you want to keep the conversation flowing ask questions that require more than a yes or no answer.

## 16 Assume he's also the lucky one

Studies show that the best chance of compatibility comes down to flirting with someone on the same level of attractiveness as you, which means if you have a low opinion of yourself you'll always feel grateful when someone talks to you, and be focused on that rather than the flirting.

## 17 Leave on a high

Also known as leave them wanting more. Sticking around until the lights come up is great if you know 100 per cent that they are interested and/or they've asked you to stick around. If not, after all the chat ask for his email/telephone number and then say you need to get back to your friends, and go. It gives him time to consider what's happened, and you time to do all your other party stuff.

## 18 Don't be a bunny boiler

You may be flirting with him but that doesn't mean he's your property and you're his girlfriend. If he gets distracted and starts looking at other women, it's not a sign to get even flirtier but a sign that he's not interested; walk away.

## 19 Take rejection on the chin

If he doesn't want to see you again don't write off the whole night as a waste of time (it hasn't been if you've had fun flirting) and don't go down the I'm-not-good-enough-for-him road. Studies show that the majority of women underestimate their attractiveness by as much as 25 per cent.

## 20 Flirt with more than one man

Not only is this great for your confidence but it's also acceptable party behaviour as long as you (a) don't lead people on; (b) don't go home with ten phone numbers (you'll be amazed at how that annoys men!); and (c) haven't spotted someone you'd like to flirt exclusively with!

# chapter 5
# *How to troubleshoot*

Ah, parties, don't you just love them, all that fun and laughter? Well, let's hope that's the way your party goes whether you're a host or a guest, because cramming 50 people into a room with free alcohol, loud music and low lighting is often more of a recipe for disaster than celebration. If you've ever had a party mishap of the emotional, physical or morning-after kind then you've come to the right place. Here's how to make sure your party life goes with a successful bang!

## *Avoiding pre-party problems*

As the host, you will find that most pre-party problems are of the organisational kind: no food, not enough drinks, no sign of your guests, blown fuses or, worse still, a double-booked venue. The good news is that all of this can be avoided with forethought and the digesting of Chapter 1. However, just as a backup, make sure you have done the following in order to help you through the night.

## Check the invitations

You're checking to make sure the date and time you've sent out is the date and time you intend to have a party. It sounds obvious but you'd be amazed at the amount of people who get this wrong and end up with an empty venue.

## Remind key players

At every party there are key players who can be relied upon to get the party going and keep it going. These are the friends who not only make sure a group of other people arrive, but also are willing to muck in and help you out. Call up these people and make sure they are coming.

## Run through your party plans with a friend

No matter how long and hard you've thought about something there will always be an essential element that you've missed. Checking your checks with a friend is the best way to spot any possible loopholes.

### Keep one room party-free

Not only will this help the next day when you want to steer clear of clutter but it will also be a welcome sanctuary at the end of the night when all you want to do is crash out. Keep this room locked if you can, to avoid revellers crashing there before you do.

### Put valuables out of harm's way

Not that your guests are going to pilfer from you, but things easily get broken when 50 people invade your space. Computers, glass, picture frames and even your best crockery should be placed out of reach.

### Clear your fridge

Not just so you can put lots of bottles in it, but also so people don't start trying to rustle up a meal when they're drunk. Guests can be notoriously bad at helping themselves to the produce in your fridge and cupboards.

### Put a lock on the bathroom door

You and your boyfriend might not mind that there isn't one there, but it's the biggest party gripe especially if your toilet happens to be further than an arm's reach away from the door.

### Check security and closing times at venues

Never just assume a venue will have a late licence and will help with the security of valuables, coats and bags. Better to ask upfront so you can tell your guests in advance what to expect.

### Check your deposit

Have you read the small print regarding what you might lose your deposit over? If not, do it now. Venues are incredibly picky, and you could well lose it over a smashed glass or broken door handle.

### Relax

It sounds stupid, but unless you want to collapse into a heap on the floor suffering from exhaustion hours before your party, it pays to relax about the event. Getting too hyped will cause an adrenaline surge that will eventually have you lying down with an ice pack on your head.

# Avoiding party problems

Hiccups of the party kind can spoil what could otherwise be a perfect night. To avoid the 'It's my party and I'll cry if

I want to' line of enjoyment, prepare for the worst and expect the best. Meaning, have a contingency plan on hand in case things get a little out of hand.

## *How not to be a wallflower*

If you're stuck talking to the yucca all night or helplessly looking at your shoes, you're in danger of becoming a wall-flower and need literally to look up and see the light. The good news is everyone feels self-conscious at a party and everyone secretly suspects everyone else is having a better time than they are. This means you really have nothing to lose by either butting into someone else's conversation (it's a party, not a meeting so nothing's that private), or going up to a complete stranger and introducing yourself.

If in doubt, start handing round cocktails or party nib-bles; it's a good icebreaker and allows you to go up and talk to people. If you do feel horribly self-conscious, think outward-focus, as in, stop looking at yourself and start looking at everyone else (for more on this hop back to Chapter 4).

## Dealing with troublesome guests/gatecrashers

One of the less savoury aspects of hosting a party is dealing with your more troublesome guests. Thankfully 90 per cent of people will fall into the dream guest variety and you'll have no problem with them. Unfortunately, that leaves 10 per cent who tend to fall into the following categories: (a) drunk and sobbing hysterically – usually to be found locked in your bathroom; (b) drunk and about to be sick – usually found in the middle of the dance-floor; (c) drunk and dangerous – usually to be found on top of a table or sitting on a window ledge; and (d) drunk and uninvited!

The first three are relatively easy to deal with because all you have to do is find the people they came with and ask them to deal with them. The last one is a more nasty variety and, if they are beyond reason, should be dealt with either with the help of large, sober men or by a quick call to your local police station (depending on the scale of the invasion).

## Being a troublesome guest

There's nothing like a bit of party booze to bring out the less pleasant parts of your personality. If you know you turn into a horror when drunk either don't get drunk (obvious, but it works) or make sure you have some good friends on hand to help steer you away from offending other guests.

*tip*

Act quickly. If you sense trouble brewing it pays to act not overact! Don't scream, get hysterical or lock yourself in the bathroom. Calmly turn up the lights, turn off the music and ask for help from other guests.

### Are you OTT?

A good way to tell if you're being too loud, too raucous or too annoying is to watch how people you don't know react to you. If they're parting like the Red Sea as you approach, finding excuses to go to the bathroom or simply just pinning themselves against a wall then you're being OTT. Likewise, if the host has to have a few words, then the chances are you are being a troublesome guest. Want to be invited again? Then tone it down by 50 per cent.

## Time please

Here's a good clue: if the lights have come up and it's not your house, then it's time to go home. Likewise, if the host is talking cabs at you, handing you your coat and turning the music off, the party is well and truly over. And as the old saying goes, it's always good to go out on a high, meaning if it's your do, don't let your party rumble on indefinitely and if it's not, don't be the last guest left standing.

If you're the host, always have a finishing point in your head and aim to start lowering the party tone about an hour before this point. Good ways to do this are to change the tempo of the music, start clearing up (a little), and make coffee; better still shout out 'Who wants a cab?'

## *Watch your drinks*

Finally, although it's a party and while I don't want to be a party pooper, one serious note to pay attention to is the area of spiked drinks. New research shows that parties are a vulnerable location for this new type of attack, so it pays to be alert. Currently most drinks that have been spiked have been found laced with the drugs Rohypnol or GHB (gamma hydroxybutyrate). The former is a strong sedative seven to ten times stronger than Valium, the other a powerful anaesthetic.

Rohypnol (the trade name for flunitrazepam, street name Roofies) not only leads to disorientation, dizziness and confusion but also has anterograde amnesia as its most significant effect. This is a condition in which events

### *Protect yourself*

To help avoid the dangers of having your drink spiked, the campaign group The Roofie Foundation suggest:

- Never leave your drink unattended.
- Be wary of accepting drinks from strangers.
- Discard your drink if it tastes odd, or has a residue in it.
- Ask for help from someone you trust 100 per cent if you feel strange, and then contact the police and request they take a urine sample for a toxicology test.

that occur while under the influence of the drug are for-gotten. Meaning, a spiked drink could leave you intensely vulnerable while giving others the impression that you are just drunk. GHB is a colourless liquid drug, which also knocks out victims and causes a similar memory loss, as well as dizziness and confusion. Both drugs are extremely potent, hard to detect in a drink, and work within 15 to 30 minutes of being administered.

# Avoiding morning-after problems

## Sex mishaps of the physical kind

The party spirit can lead to all kinds of things post-party and even if you're usually 100 per cent careful, mishaps of the sexual kind can easily happen.

If you have had unprotected sex, there are two methods of preventing pregnancy you should know about:

## The emergency pill

This is available from your local chemist, your doctor and family planning clinics. Available if unprotected sex occurs within 72 hours (three days). Unlike PC4, the old emergency pill, which contained four pills, the newest pill – Levonelle-2 – has only two. The benefits of this pill are:

- It doesn't make you feel sick or cause you to throw up.
- It's also 95 per cent effective and holds no health risks. This pill stops conception happening (it won't work if you are already pregnant) and is not the same as the abortion pill, which is not available over the counter.

### *IUD*

If you've waited beyond 72 hours but the event occurred less than five days ago, an IUD can be inserted by a doctor into the uterus to prevent the lining of the womb from thickening and therefore halt conception. This is an effective post-sex method and it's contraceptive value can last three years (or you can have it removed again).

## *Sex mishaps of the emotional kind*

Waking up to a one-night stand is more common than people think and is often fuelled by a mixture of drink and the party spirit. If you've had a one-night stand, as tempting as it is to go down the 'I must beat myself up about this' route, don't! The fact is sexual decisions happen for all kinds of reasons and it doesn't make you a vile person if you've done something you usually avoid like the plague. Of course, much of this depends on who you have slept with – hopefully it's not your boss, your best friend's boyfriend or an ex you've just spent six months trying to get rid of. If it is, you probably need a whole different kind of book to help out!

### *Embarrassing morning-after revelations*

(Also known as: how to survive your party performance.) The good news is, I doubt there is one person who hasn't done something embarrassing at a party. Whether it's dancing on a table, falling over drunk, making an inappropriate pass at someone or even thinking it's a great idea to whip off your top for a photo opportunity!

If any of these ring a familiar bell then it's likely your friends have never let you forget the time when you did X! As tempting as it is to hang your head in shame and let the cold shiver of embarrassment wash over you again and again and again, make sure you get your party performance in perspective. Life is short – if you had a good time then there's no point in ruining the event with regrets of the I-wish-I-hadn't-done-that variety. Of course, there are things to learn from (such as rude photos) and things to revel in (dancing on a table) and the rest is just the party spirit.

## *You look like a morning-after disaster*

Even though you may have spent the majority of your pre-party days getting your body party-ready, most of us wake up the morning after the night before looking like an extra from a horror film. If you're bleary eyed and splotchy here's how to combat it without frightening your neighbours (for more on this see Chapter 2):

### Bleary eyes

Nothing beats cotton wool pads soaked in tepid water for de-puffing your eyes. Moisten the pads with water, lie back and gently press them over your eyes for ten minutes. To get rid of dark circles, use concealer along the bottom edge of the circles (use your ring finger, as this applies just the right kind of pressure you need).

### Bad breath

This is the result of party snacks and alcohol (the dehydrating effects of alcohol also dry up your saliva). The best cure is peppermint tea and lots of water. Food-wise, stick to plain foods and fruit to help cleanse the palate.

### Patchy skin

To help the body combat the effects of a hangover and lack of sleep blood is diverted away from your skin causing patchiness. Help yourself by massaging your face along your eyebrow line, along your jaw line and your cheeks. Pay particular attention to your eye sockets and forehead.

### Headache

Apart from drinking a good few litres of water to re-hydrate your body, opt for a head massage. Using your fingers, manipulate and rub your scalp, temples and brow line, concentrating on areas that feel tight and tense.

# The clearing up guide

Throwing a party always seems like such a fantastic idea until you're faced with a mountain of washing up, a carpet that probably needs to be shampooed ten times and enough rubbish bags to fill your front room. Ways to make it bearable if you can't afford professional cleaners are:

## Do a little before you go to bed

It sounds a horrible thing, but you'll be glad in the morning, and you should still have a few people around to help. Good suggestions for night clearing include throwing out all half-eaten food, chucking half-full cans of drink down the sink, emptying ashtrays and throwing out anything that smells.

## Get the friends who stayed over to do it

This doesn't mean languishing on the sofa shouting out instructions, but tactfully asking for help. Remember these people are doing it out of the kindness of their hearts, meaning, don't give them horrible jobs, don't yell at them if they don't do it right and reward them for their efforts. Good rewards include the promise of food, more drink and even help when they next have a party.

## Have a system

Whether you're an expert or not, it pays to have a system when you're clearing up, especially if you're rubbish at it. Be logical, and clear up all the debris first – this is the paper plates, glasses, bottles and leftovers – before you do the more heavy-duty stuff. Apart from helping you to see that there is an end to the mess, moving all the waste stuff to one side actually enables you to see what needs to be cleaned, washed, wiped and hosed down with bleach. Be sure to look under chairs and tables, and in the rooms that have supposedly been shut off to guests.

## Do it in one day

Tempting, as it is to leave it for a few days, the longer you leave party stuff hanging about, the more work it will take to clear up. Clean up immediately and you won't be sorry. Also worth noting is that anything that doesn't get cleaned up within a week tends to be still there two months later.

## Don't be afraid to ask for help

What are good girl friends for apart from to help in a crisis, and what's a domestic clean up if not a crisis? Help make it a pleasant experience by turning up the music, having regular rest breaks and dissecting who did what and with whom the night before.

# 20 *ways* to make your party go with a bang

**1 Have mini-cab numbers on hand**
Handier than you'll ever know. Apart from helping you to offload reluctant-to-leave guests, having two or three numbers on hand will save you fumbling about in the kitchen drawers at 2.00 a.m. Call the cab companies beforehand and see who is most likely to have five or more cabs on their books in the early hours. Better still, get some quotes for various areas so you can let your guests know in advance.

**2 Have a first-aid kit handy**
It's amazing what people will do when they are drunk and disorderly, so it does pay to have a first-aid kit for emergency moments. Good stock products are: painkillers for headaches, plasters for cuts, cotton wool and antiseptic. A spare needle and thread are also handy for clothes that fall apart.

**3 Keep a spare outfit/T-shirts for friends**
It doesn't take much to ruin a party outfit, so unless you want half-naked guests staggering about, keep three clean T-shirts handy for guests whose clothes don't make it through the night.

**4 Be ready to be master of all trades**
Waitress/bar tender/DJ and agony aunt – if you're the host, this is your job too. It's all part of being Uber-hostess and will up your party-throwing status if you can happily do all of the above and still find time to mingle with guests.

**5 Let people remember you for the right reasons**
It's easy when you're throwing a party to fall into policeman/mother status and constantly tell people not to turn the music up or not to put their drinks on bare tabletops and instantly wipe up spillages at their feet. But unless your house has fallen out of the pages of an interior magazine (in which case it's probably

best not to have a party there) you need to relax.

## 6 Don't get pulled into someone else's drama

There's always going to be someone crying in the bathroom, having a fight with his or her partner or fighting over someone with his or her best friend at a party! Unless these people are wrestling on the dance-floor or about to fall through a window, or in danger of killing each other, let them work it out or else your whole night will be taken up with them.

## 7 Have enough of the basics

Basics means soft drinks, mixers, ice, glasses and bin bags – everything else you can do without, send out for or beg from a neighbour.

## 8 Make sure you've alerted your neighbours

If you haven't invited them it pays to let them know that it's going to be a little noisy until late. Make them feel better by promising to turn things down when it

gets too loud and maybe even throw in an invitation – what can it hurt?

## 9 Have a back-up music system (even if it's just a radio)

Electrical equipment has a funny way of breaking down just when you need it, so for the sake of the party spirit always have music back up. People can party without drink and food, but not without music.

## 10 Know whom to call if disaster strikes

Not just the police but workmen for broken windows, the local pharmacy for cuts and bruises, and even the local pizza man for food top ups.

## 11 Don't try to do it all on your own

Simply because you don't have to.

## 12 Expect someone may need to stay over

OK, everyone said they were going home and/or you didn't offer to put anyone up, but expect at least one couple to stay over. Whether this is down to over-drinking or not being able to get a cab, be prepared so you won't have to search for spare blankets at 3.00 a.m.

## 13 Keep some food and drink back for later

This is a good tip if you have hoards of hungry guests descending on you for more than five hours. Most food and drink naturally seems to dwindle after three hours, so make sure you bring out your party food and drink in batches. Forty-five minutes after the start for the first batch of food, and about three hours after the party has moved into full swing.

## 14 Have morning-after supplies

You'll be grateful for this when you wake up at 8.00 a.m. starving. To make sure your guests don't eat your supplies, keep them well hidden and out of arm's reach.

## 15 Prepare for the worst, expect the best

It sounds a depressing thought but it isn't. Roughly speaking this means – plan as if something is going to go wrong, that is, know what to do if the roof falls in, but assume it won't!

## 16 Don't expect perfection

The number-one party mistake is to expect and want everything to be perfect. Perfection only exists in the mind and no one, least of all your guests, care if the table is crooked and the wine cost you a month's wages!

## 17 Be a social butterfly

This means, make sure you talk to everyone at least once before you hone in on the man you fancy and stand flirting with him all night. It may be a bore, but it's party etiquette to at least talk to your guests.

## 18 Don't worry about your guests

Are people having a good time? Well, that's not your responsibility. As guests, people have to make a party work for them. If they're crying in a corner or wandering around looking forlorn, the chances are their behaviour has nothing to do with your party.

## 19 Take time to enjoy yourself

Don't be too rigorous about how the party should look, when people should eat and what music should be played where and when. If you spend too long worrying about these things you won't enjoy a moment of your party.

## 20 Let go of the control button

Also known as just relax and enjoy. If you've organised everything to the last detail, said hello to your guests, fed them and basically made every effort to have your room looking fantastic, it's time to actually enjoy the event you've spent weeks planning.

# chapter 6
# How to feel better fast

If you're someone who rarely feels alive, never mind happy, the morning after the night before, then this is the chapter for you. This is where we show you how to make sure the party life of high heels, excess alcohol, rubbish food and accidental bumps and lumps doesn't ruin the rest of your normal life.

## The lazy girl's guide to boozing

If you're anything like the average woman out there, then the chances are parties are a good time to drink your entire monthly unit allowance of alcohol in one go. Known fondly as binge drinking, this is a good way to throw your guts up, do something you will regret, wake up embarrassed and/or end up in hospital. Studies all over the world show binge drinking ups your chances of risking unprotected sex, helps you gain weight and leads to large errors of judgement that can cause numerous accidents.

So step one in lazy girl drinking is to choose not to overdo it. If the thought of past embarrassments doesn't stop you, think for a second what all this drink does to your body.

Firstly, a few drinks may leave you feeling happy, but take one too many and this will soon change to superconfidence, in other words a lack of normal judgement. So your normal sensible reactions, which stop you running naked down the street, will disappear. This happens because alcohol is absorbed directly into the bloodstream and stays in your body until the liver burns it up. As this happens slowly – at the rate of one unit an hour – you'll also have impaired judgement for this time (so if you drink five vodkas and two glasses of wine you'll stay intoxicated for seven hours).

## The effects of drinking

Just two glasses of wine and two vodkas in one night will do the following:

- Reduce your chance of having a decent orgasm. This is because alcohol lowers your arousal levels and reaction times.
- Increase your body weight. Four drinks will give you the munchies at midnight, meaning it's chips/pizza/kebabs on the way home. This is around 2,000 extra calories and can add 225g/½lb of fat to your body.
- Give you blurry vision: alcohol paralyses eye muscles so that you can't focus, and also stops co-ordination in the brain, which means you're more likely to fall down, get run over or cause an accident.
- Give you stomach problems, including constipation and diarrhoea, as alcohol can inflame and ulcerate the lining of the digestive tract.

## What's a unit?

A unit is a standard measure of alcohol (about 8g or 10ml by volume of pure alcohol per unit). The current weekly level for women is 14 units, but this is a standard guide so it may be too high for you, especially if you are small and weigh less than all your friends. Sadly, units apply only to pub measures, meaning your party measures will be higher because you're doing the pouring. A regular unit equals half a pint of normal-strength beer, a small glass of wine or a standard measure of spirits.

## *fact*

The body gets rid of roughly one unit of alcohol per hour. Therefore, if you start drinking in the evening it will take you until 2.00 a.m., at least, until you sober up after six or seven (measured) glasses of wine.

## *Hangover helper*

Not all drinks are created equal. Here are the choices most likely to give you a headache the morning after the night before.

| Drink | Units | Hangover Rating (per measure) |
|---|---|---|
| Cream liqueurs | 1 | low |
| Gin and tonic | 1 | low to medium |
| Lager | 1 | low to medium |
| Alcopops | 1.5 | medium to high |
| Champagne | 1.5 | medium to high |
| Red wine (large) | 2 | high |
| White wine | 2 | medium |
| Cocktails | 2–4 | extremely high |

## *The lazy girl's guide to safer drinking*

Having overloaded you with all the science and anatomical stuff, here's what you really need to know when it comes to drinking and having a good time:

1. Always pour your own drinks so that you know what you're drinking and exactly how much.

2. Avoid the punch/cocktails/offers of drinks – unless you know what's in them.

3. Aim to drink one alcoholic drink an hour and have a soft drink in between each measure of alcohol.

4. Eat something before you start drinking – you'll drink less and have less of a hangover.

5. If you're too drunk, always get someone sober to pour you a drink.

6. Don't match a man drink for drink – men can drink more than women can before getting drunk owing to their size and body make up.

7. Read the alcohol percentage strength on beer and wine bottles – a strong percentage equals two units, not one!

8. Fizzy alcohol/wine and alcopops will get you drunk faster because the bubbles speed the alcohol into your bloodstream.

9. Know how you're getting home before you start drinking heavily.

10. If you're on medication, watch what you drink; certain drugs can mix badly with alcohol.

11. If you feel at all ill, tell someone (especially if you don't think

you've drunk that much) – passing out and being sick is a ticket to your local hospital emergency room.

12. Stop drinking when you consciously think 'Oops I think I'm drunk', because you are!

13. If you want to beat a hangover, don't do hair of the dog – it doesn't work!

14. Always add more mixers than alcohol to your drink so you get drunk at a slower rate.

## *fact*

Your drink is stronger than you think. The strength of drinks has risen in the last ten years. The alcohol level in wine is now 13 per cent rather than 9 per cent, raising the unit level to nine in a bottle of wine (not six).

## *How to tell if you're drinking too much*

You don't have to drink a lot to end up with a killer hangover. If you answer yes to two or more of the following questions, you are drinking too much:

### 1. You boast that you can hold your alcohol.

Downing ten drinks or more without getting drunk, doesn't mean you aren't affected by alcohol. It's more likely your body's adjusted itself to large amounts of alcohol, meaning it now takes more to get you drunk. Bad news for your liver, kidneys and brain cells.

### 2. You regularly have no recollection of what happened when you were drunk.

Again, bad news – blackouts and memory loss mean you've effectively shut down your brain with alcohol.

### 3. You often say you should cut down on your drinking.

Most of us know (even if we won't admit it) if we're drinking too much. If you feel you are, then you are!

### 4. You feel annoyed when people tell you to cut down.

Feeling defensive about your alcohol intake is also a sure sign that you need to cut down.

### 5. You use alcohol to get happy/relaxed/confident.

We all use alcohol as a prop; however, if it's a constant one, then you need to look at other ways to combat your weak spots.

### 6. You can't go out and not drink.

This is the perfect test to see if you really have a grasp on your drinking or not.

### 7. You've hurt yourself on more than two occasions when drunk.

Bad judgement, lack of co-ordination – this can occur with just five units of alcohol.

### 8. You often have to take a day off work and/or lie in bed after drinking.

A hangover is effectively alcohol poisoning. The more you're unable to perform everyday functions, the higher the level of poisoning.

### 9. You think alcohol is good for you.

While studies show one drink a day is good for your heart and ups levels of good cholesterol (HDL) the protective effects stop as soon as you drink more than two drinks.

### 10. You think you're safe because you never mix your drinks.

While mixing the grape and the grain will give you a nasty headache owing to congeners (chemicals found in alcohol which irritate the brain) in the beer and wine, there's no evidence that this makes you drunk quicker. The only reason mixing results in a hangover is that you are more likely to drink more units by mixing your drinks.

*fact*

You'll get drunk faster than your boyfriend: women absorb a third more alcohol than a man of the same size, owing to less effective stomach-enzyme activity.

## Beat your hangovers the lazy way

We've all been there: the spinning room, the thumping headache and the rising nausea – yes it's the hangover from hell and it's happening to you.

Hangovers occur for two reasons: one, you're dehydrated because the alcohol in your body has been acting like a diuretic all night which means you have had to keep going to the toilet; and two, drinks such as red wine and whisky switch on the brain's pain receptors causing that painful stabbing behind your eyes. You then feel lacking in energy because levels of insulin have been produced in the body as a response to the sugar you've taken in from the alcohol, this means you also probably feel faint and hungry. Luckily you can avoid the nastiness by following a more sensible approach to party drinking.

### Eat before you party

A full stomach slows down alcohol absorption; so good foods to eat are ones that are easily digested. A piece of toast, a sandwich with a light filling, a small bowl of pasta, and yoghurt all protect the stomach lining; plus, they won't stop you getting into your glad rags or give you that full protruding-belly feeling. Foods that are processed or high in sugar will take the alcohol with them into the bloodstream, and so junk food should be avoided at all costs prior to a party.

### Take your vitamins

Antioxidants are particularly adept at fighting off alcohol damage and protecting your liver. They also stop your brain cells being killed off by weekend binges. Found in green leafy vegetables and fruit, you should aim to get ample amounts of vitamins A, C and E in the days before a big night out.

On the night itself consider stocking up on vitamin C as this is used up in huge amounts to break down alcohol in the body.

### Buy some milk thistle and artichoke

Milk thistle and artichoke are great herbal remedies, which help detoxify the liver and improve digestive function. It is hailed as a natural hangover cure. For optimum results take a dose before you go out and one when you come back in, and then another the following morning.

### Get enough H₂O

Before you drink anything, drink a pint of water. Besides stopping you from overdoing it in the first hour (the time when most people get drunk) it will help you to not get dehydrated. Before you go to sleep make yourself drink another pint of water, again to stop dehydration. This will also help rid your body of the toxin acetaldehyde, which is released by the liver when alcohol is broken down. It is this toxin that leads to a thumping head.

### Forgo the fry-up

You may wake up craving fried food, junk food and doughnuts for comfort reasons, but cramming all that fat into your body will just make you feel ill and hinder an already flagging digestive system. Your aim should be to stabilise your blood sugar, so you need to eat small portions of healthy food frequently: think about weak tea, toast and honey, and even porridge or cereal.

### Have a prairie oyster

This is a raw egg swallowed whole (no oyster involved – the name comes from the slang for a bull's testicle). Supposedly works because of a chemical found in eggs known as cystine, which helps metabolise alcohol in the body; although you're really better off having some scrambled eggs on toast!

### Sip fizzy or flat cola or ginger ale

This is an excellent cure for feeling sick. It's said to settle the stomach and get rid of waves of nausea.

### Give yourself time to get over it

The best cure in the world – because if you rest up and avoid alcohol for a few days, you'll give your body a chance to jettison the excess alcohol swilling around your gut. Eat healthily and give yourself a decent night's sleep and the morning after The Morning After you'll feel fine.

### Think about your stomach

One horrible side effect of a hangover is acid reflux, also known as indigestion, the 'burning' feeling in your throat and stomach. If you don't fancy taking an antacid in the morning, use your pillows to raise your chest and head to 15cm (6in) above your stomach and avoid food two hours before going to bed.

### Take some exercise

Not of the intense aerobic kind (which will probably make you pass out) but of the fresh air and walks kind. This will not only help to clear your head and speed up your by-now sluggish metabolism but it will also help your body to detoxify at a slightly faster rate.

## Save your looks from alcohol

1 **Slap on the moisturiser:** your skin is crying out for a drink, so apply lashings to your face and balm to your lips the morning after, and if you're capable the night before.

2 **Look after your eyes:** de-bag with cold tea bags over the eyes and use eye drops to refresh and rehydrate the whites of your eyes.

3 **Avoid a face full of make-up:** apart from making you look like the Bride of Frankenstein, your make-up is likely to be a shade too dark, as blood is circulated away from the skin to

help your body cope with the effects of too much booze. Go for a hat, sunglasses and lip gloss if you have to venture out.
**4 Tie your hair up:** alcohol excretes through your pores, so hair may feel greasy and lank. Tie it up or pull it back to avoid having to feel it round your face all day.

# The painkiller guide for party mishaps

Forget the excessive drinking; parties are dangerous things and you don't need to be drunk to come home with bumps, bruises and a few nasty aches and pains. If you're the worse for wear the morning after here's how to feel better fast.

***Problem:*** you slipped on the dance floor.
One minute you were looking like an extra from a J. Lo video, the next you were flat on your back – not so funny the morning after when your back and neck hurt.

***Perfect painkiller:*** Ibuprofen.

***Why it works:*** Ibuprofen has excellent anti-inflammatory properties, which means it will kill pain fast. The joy of this painkiller is it also comes in a topical cream, so if you want extra pain relief, massage a small amount into the problem area. This will lower the temperature of the area and help relax your sore muscles.

*How quickly it works:* a normal dosage of 400mg will take an hour to get into your bloodstream; although certain brands (fast acting ones) only take 20 minutes to ease the ache. Long-lasting Ibuprofen is especially good if you want to get a good night's sleep as one dose lasts for over four hours.

*How long it lasts:* for four hours, but never take Ibuprofen on an empty stomach, as it can irritate and upset the stomach lining.

*Alternative help:* place a hot-water bottle under your back and stay off your feet until the ache has been soothed.


*Problem:* your feet hurt from wearing killer heels all night. They may not be a smart option but they're damn sexy – shame the morning after you can't even walk to the bathroom without feeling as if sharp nails are being pushed into your foot.

*Perfect painkiller:* a cream with lavender and mint.

*Why it works:* lavender helps relax aching muscles and mint cools down hot, sore feet. The best way to apply TLC to battered feet is to massage in the cream for five minutes, and then to sit with your feet up, which stops fluids pooling in the feet (the result of standing up for long periods of time). This then reduces pressure on the nerve endings and stops foot pain instantly.

*How quickly it works:* within five minutes.

*How long it lasts:* until you don those killer heels again.

*Alternative help:* massage the balls of your feet, as this is where all your body weight lands up when you wear heels over 5cm (2in) high.

*Problem:* you're having a major throwing-up incident. Amazingly, a diet of crisps, chips and white wine will do little for the state of your stomach.

*Perfect painkiller:* oral electrolyte powder sachets available from all pharmacists.

*Why it works:* standard dehydration sachets replace fluids and salts lost through hangovers, diarrhoea and being sick, and so ease stomach pain.

*How quickly it works:* sachets should be taken as soon as you have been sick, and will work within 30 minutes. Paracetamol takes one hour to hit your bloodstream and works pretty instantly if you can keep it down.

*How long it lasts:* three hours.

# fact

You'll get a drink problem faster than a man. It takes up to ten years of heavy drinking for a susceptible man to become dependent, but only three to four for a female.

*Alternative help:* drink lots of water to rehydrate your body and don't eat anything for 24 hours to give your stomach a rest.

*Problem:* you ache all over.
Party all night with little or no sleep and you're asking for major aches and pains.

*Perfect painkiller:* aspirin.

*Why it works:* aspirin is a good all-rounder on the painkiller front; it is anti-inflammatory, like Ibuprofen, plus it can help reduce fever and headaches fast.

*How quickly it works:* normal aspirin works within 40–60 minutes, but if you're in pain soluble aspirin is your best bet, as it will work within 30 minutes. This is because dissolvable painkillers get into your bloodstream much faster. Aspirin can irritate the stomach lining, so don't take it on an empty stomach.

*How long it lasts:* up to four hours.

*Alternative help:* have a long warm bath (not hot or you'll pass out with your hangover) and then go to bed.

*Problem:* you have a hangover headache.
Dull, throbbing headache, piercing pain, light sensitivity? No, you're not dying, you've got a hangover headache.

*Perfect painkiller:* codeine with paracetamol.

*Why it works:* codeine is an opiate painkiller with a stronger kick, which equals zero pain. However, it's not available over the counter, but you can buy it mixed with other painkillers, such as paracetamol. One nasty side effect that should be noted is overuse leads to constipation.

*How quickly it works:* it takes 40 minutes to one hour to get into your system.

*How long it lasts:* four hours, depending on the strength of the tablet, so check your doses.

*Alternative help:* lots of water and sleep.

*Problem:* you have a few noticeable cuts and bruises.
Mysterious bruises on your legs, a scrape on your knee? Here's how to soothe your war-torn party skin.

*Perfect painkiller:* herbal remedies, arnica, witch-hazel and echinacea. Arnica will help bring out bruises and heal the skin, and echinacea cream will soothe, while witch-hazel promotes healing.

*Why it works:* arnica taken as a cream or tablet is known to reduce inflammation and get rid of a bruise faster than usual. Echinacea also has an active ingredient, which is anti-bacterial, and promotes fast wound-healing on minor cuts. Witch-hazel is a natural antiseptic with strong anti-viral properties – especially good if you happened to come face to face with the pavement last night.

*How quickly it works:* the creams soothe within five minutes.

*Alternative treatment:* as above.

*Problem:* you're having chest pains.
Even though it's very important to see your doctor if you have any chest pain, relax, it's unlikely to be a heart attack. The pains could be fibrillation – or irregular heartbeats brought on by excessive caffeine and alcohol intake (how many lattes have you had today?), a hangover and over-exertion on the dance floor.

*Perfect painkiller:* If you're given the all clear by the doctor for heart problems, it's probably indigestion. This feels like a sharp stabbing pain at the breastbone (your stomach's higher than you think) and is easily alleviated with over-the-counter anti-acids.

*Alternative treatment:* fizzy ginger ale or peppermint tea, to calm you down and soothe your tummy.

*Problem:* you hit your head.
If you were knocked out for longer than a few seconds, are having vision or memory problems and/or have been sick and feel dizzy, then you need to seek medical advice as soon as possible, as it could be concussion.

*Perfect painkiller:* If you're told you are ok by the doctor, it could just be a bump. If you just have a sore head (with none of the above symptoms) take Ibuprofen as it has excellent anti-inflammatory properties, which will stop the pain.

*Alternative treatment:* lie down and put a cold compress on your head.

*Problem:* you've sprained your ankle.
Running in heels is an extreme sport, especially when drunk. If the pain practically makes you pass out and the joint has swelled, or if it is discoloured or twisted and can't be touched, go to the hospital – it could be a sprain or fracture.

*Perfect painkiller:* don't take anything, as only an X-ray will give you the correct diagnosis.

*Alternative treatment:* see a doctor first, and if he tells you to rest, practise the RICE technique: Rest, Ice, Compression and Elevation (that is, rest your leg on something).

***Problem:*** you've got backache.

If the pain is located on both sides of your back, and you experience pain when you pee (or can't pee) and feel sick, it could be a kidney infection. However, if you've been wearing high heels and/or have been dancing all night, the ache in your spine will be caused by bad posture resulting from your pelvis being thrown forwards when you walked and danced.

***Perfect painkiller:*** Ibuprofen and a hot water bottle on your back.

***Alternative treatment:*** see an osteopath and strengthen your lower back with Pilates and yoga once you're better.

***Problem:*** diarrhoea.

It's likely you're run down from too much partying, not enough sleep and a diet of midnight kebabs.

***Perfect painkillers:*** don't take anti-diarrhoea drugs, as it's a case of better out than in. Diarrhoea should clear up in

## fact

The average drinker today consumes 150 per cent more alcohol than 50 years ago.

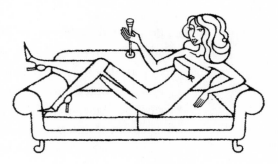

two days if you avoid spicy foods, fatty and dairy foods and alcohol. Drink lots of water to replace lost fluids.

*Alternative treatment:* let it all out (as above).

*Problem:* you're feeling dizzy.
If it lasts for over five days or is accompanied by fainting and vomiting see your doctor; otherwise, if you've been drinking heavily and burning the candle at both ends it could be fatigue or an inner-ear infection brought on by all your bad habits.

*Perfect painkiller:* get eight hours sleep a night, eat properly, give up alcohol for a week and then see how you feel.

*Alternative treatment:* give up your partying ways.

*Problem:* you're stuffed up.
When it comes to unloading, what's normal varies from person to person, but constipation is usually the result of a poor diet, not enough water and too much booze.

*Perfect painkiller:* eat plenty of fibre-rich foods, but don't add bran to foods. On the whole you should be aiming for at least 18–30g (¾–1oz) of fibre a day, and 2 litres (3¼ pints) of water (more if you exercise, and drink coffee and alcohol). Fibre-rich foods are vegetables, fruit (especially dried fruit) and whole grains, such as wholemeal bread, and brown rice and pasta. Over-the-counter laxatives help, but also try apricots, prunes, linseeds and/or flaxseeds, as these work as natural laxatives.

*Why it works:* fibre alleviates constipation, as it absorbs water while it passes through the digestive system with waste. Providing you are drinking plenty of liquids, the fibre becomes soft in the gut making it easy and comfortable to go to the toilet.

*How quickly it works:* within a day.

*Alternative treatment:* try massaging your tummy, in a circular clockwise motion only, starting from the right side of your groin and moving over to the left side. This will help stimulate the colon to move waste along.

# Kick your bad party habits

If you're planning on having some post-party energy, here's what you should be thinking about.

## What are you eating?

If your meals leave you feeling bloated, overly full, lethargic and more like a stuffed turkey than the one on your mum's Christmas table, it's time to rearrange how you eat.

Glasses of wine, mince pies, crisps and nuts for your evening meal is a ticket to bloating. Luckily, balancing the good times with healthy eating is relatively easy.

### Step one: avoid big gaps between your meals

Food fatigue happens for a variety of reasons, the most common of which are fluctuating blood sugar levels. This occurs when your body converts the junk food you eat into sugar too quickly. If too much sugar is released into the body in one go by either waiting too long to eat between meals or by eating foods such as chocolate, fatty foods and/or drinking too much coffee, tea or alcohol, the following happens:

Too much insulin is released to combat the sugar levels in the body. This causes your blood sugar levels to rise and then to fall rapidly, leading to a quick burst of energy followed by the inevitable exhaustion, anxiety, irritability and hunger pangs. Luckily, balancing your blood sugar is relatively easy. Aim to eat little and often during the day, and never wait more than three hours to eat something. Sometimes just an oatcake or a piece of fruit between meals will be enough to keep your energy even all day.

### Step two: eat a healthy breakfast and lunch

If you suffer from mid-afternoon slumps after a heavy night partying, think about what you're eating when you first wake up. A breakfast of toast or cereal and a lunch

# fact

It pays to make healthy choices. A Harvard University study of 65,000 women found those with diets high in simple carbohydrates, junk food and fizzy drinks upped their risk of developing adult onset diabetes by a mammoth 250 per cent.

made up of sandwiches or pasta is very taxing on the body's hormone levels. Starchy refined carbohydrates like these are processed too quickly in the body, which means an instant high followed by an inevitable mid-afternoon low. Excessive carbohydrates in any form without any protein are the kiss of death.

To eat wisely eat complex carbohydrates, such as oats and rye breads, and a wide variety of vegetables and fruit. A good lunch would be foods such as chicken, Caesar salad, and/or a tuna niçoise salad. Sandwiches can also be eaten, but in a different way to keep your energy up: the filling should always outweigh the bread. This will keep your energy up all afternoon. For those reaching for an afternoon snack – beware the mandatory chocolate bar and packet of crisps. Better options are a packet of unsalted almonds, fruit such as apples and pears, raw vegetables, or even a small tub of cottage cheese or hummus.

### Step three: be wary of ready-made drinks

Surprisingly a shop-bought smoothie or fruit juice may not give you the health boost you need. Ready-made smoothies, in particular, have had all the natural fruit fibre taken out; meaning all you're drinking is pure fruit sugar.

To make a healthy home-made smoothie out of a shop-bought one, add a small tub of natural bio yoghurt and mix fruit juices with water.

As for coffee and fizzy drinks, these stimulants initiate an express delivery of energy to the body, equalling a parallel express low with irritability thrown in. If you really can't give coffee up, cut down the number of cups you drink a day. Drink coffee before lunch to stop your body crashing. The recommended daily allowance of coffee is around 300mg; a normal mug contains approximately 150mg of coffee (instant contains 100mg). If you have one for breakfast, one at 11.00 a.m. and one after lunch, you're already scoring 450mg, and that's if you've stuck to a medium-sized mug.

## How are you sleeping?

A good night's sleep is essential for mental health; this is because while we're sleeping we go through a series of restorative chemical changes that recharge the brain. Unfortunately, overstimulation of the brain through alcohol, late nights, takeaway foods at 2.00 a.m. means you'll *tip*

Get more sleep. Research from the University of Chicago Sleep Unit shows that a lack of sleep not only boosts levels of the stress hormone cortisol, but also weakens your immunity and increases stores of body fat, leaving you feeling bloated, irritable and unable to sleep.

miss out on stages three to five of sleep – deep sleep and REM (rapid eye movement) sleep – both of which are essential for your psychic regeneration.

Help yourself by:

**Maintaining healthy sleep patterns** on the nights you are not partying. Just three late nights in two weeks will essentially rob you of a whole night's sleep.

**Not sleeping in too late.** You can't play catch-up with sleep; it just disrupts your body's sleep patterns even more than usual. Feel better by going to bed an hour earlier the next night, rather than staying in bed three hours later the next morning.

**Not drinking too much alcohol** and eating too much fatty food before you go to bed, as this will hinder your digestive system and interfere with REM sleep – resulting in you waking up exhausted.

**Take some vitamin B5 (pantothenic acid).** This is the perfect antidote for too much cortisol (the stress hormone) from the adrenal glands. Siberian ginseng and liquorice can also help if you have adrenaline overload.

## How much are you smoking?

We all know smoking is bad for your health, but binge smoking (where you only smoke when you're out) is bad news for your looks and health simply because you'll probably smoke more in one night than the average smoker will in one week. Nicotine also depletes the body's stores of vitamin C, which is essential for maintaining healthy-looking skin. Worse still, smoking can inhibit the functioning of immune cells, which can lead to an increase in the incidence of colds and infections as well as an irritation of the digestive tract. The result of this is your post-party effects could well last two weeks more than they would usually have to.

### How to give up binge smoking

- Spot your triggers for smoking. How many drinks do you need before you beg for a cigarette? Stop before you reach this point, or at least sober up for half an hour before you get another drink.
- Put something else in your mouth when you feel like a cigarette: ice cubes, peanuts or a soft drink.

- Remind yourself that every cigarette counts, so if you've smoked ten, the eleventh butt will make a difference.
- Don't fool yourself that you're not a smoker. If you smoke 30 a week (even if it's in one go) you're a smoker and need all the usual help in order to quit.
- Above all, remember that although the more you smoke the greater the risk, just one or two cigarettes a day are more than enough to cause lung cancer (smoking-related lung cancer has risen by 70 per cent in under 15 years).

## Give up binge smoking (or even smoking)...

... and within:

**Twenty minutes** your blood pressure will fall.

**Eight hours** the levels of poisonous carbon monoxide in your blood will drop to normal.

**Two days** your chances of a heart attack will have decreased and your sense of smell will be returning.

**Three days** your lung airways will start to relax.

**Two weeks** your circulation will improve.

**One month** sinus congestion and fatigue will decrease.

**Two months** your lung function will start to improve.

**Six months** your overall energy will increase.

**One year** premature wrinkling will decrease and the risk of coronary heart disease will have dropped to half of that of a smoker.

**Three to five years** your risk of lung cancer will have reduced to normal.

**Ten years** your health risks will have dropped to the same as a non-smoker and your chance of lung cancer will be similar to that of a non-smoker.

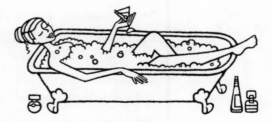

# 20 ways
# to feel better fast

## 1 Go to bed an hour earlier every night for a week

Don't underestimate the restorative power of sleep. If you're feeling blue, fatigued, miserable, hungover or near to flu, then gently adding the equivalent of a whole night's sleep to your life (one hour extra a night for a week = one night's sleep) can help you feel better faster than a painkiller and a holiday.

## 2 Think about your biorhythms

This is your recurring pattern of natural body states. We're all programmed to nap around eight hours after waking. Unfortunately, your boss won't be very understanding if he finds you sleeping at your desk, so a better option is to push yourself to be active when you're tired because physical activity will rev you up, stretch out cramped muscles and rejuvenate you.

## 3 Take a nap before you go out

Studies from the New York University Sleep Disorders Center advocate power naps as a powerful way to combat fatigue. However, nap for only ten minutes; any more than this and you'll end up in a deep sleep and stop any chance of waking up refreshed.

## 4 Take some deep breaths

Sitting slumped over your desk all day and on your sofa equals bad posture, which in turn equals shallow breathing and more tiredness. If you yawn a lot (yawning is the body's mechanism to draw in more oxygen), think about how you do everyday things such as sitting, standing and walking. Try breathing deeply at your desk for ten counts – your stomach should push out as you breathe in and pull in as you breathe out.

## 5 Have a curry to beat a hangover

The ingredients found in most curries – chilli, garlic, ginger and turmeric – are good for sweating, detoxing the body and relieving nausea. Keep clear of the creamy curries, as these will just upset an already upset stomach; stick to dry curries with plain rice.

**6 Cut your unit intake in half**
You can drink yourself young and you can drink yourself old, and the difference is slim. Have one or two small drinks a day and you'll feel fine; have three or more large drinks and you'll have killer hangovers and the face of a 50 year old.

**7 Drink more water between your alcoholic choices**
Water will help flush out a variety of toxins from your body, helping you to feel healthier for longer (and have less of a hangover the next day). Drinking two large glasses of water post-partying and before sleeping can also help you wake up with less of a heavy head.

**8 Count your colds**
Are you always ill or feeling like you're coming down with something? Hypochondria aside, it could be your partying habit. Your immune system will basically conk out if you consistently deny it healthy food, sleep and fresh air.

**9 Put your relationship before the booze**
Watch what your habits are doing to your love life. If you won't cut down for your health, cut down for love. Heavy drinkers and party animals are twice as likely to have a marriage that heads for the divorce courts owing to drink-fuelled fights, lack of sex and irritable mornings after.

**10 Use the right feel-better techniques**
It's a myth that black coffee will cure your hangover and sober you up. It will only add to your dehydration problem. Meanwhile, research in the UK shows that within 30 minutes of drinking a large cappuccino or expresso, the flow of blood to the brain is reduced by 10–20 per cent. Which is why you get that shaky, sweaty feeling with too many lattes.

## 11 Eat five portions of fruit and vegetables a day

Only 13 per cent of men and 15 per cent of women have their recommended daily allowance of fruit and vegetables, which are full of powerful antioxidants that help fight free radicals found in alcohol and polluted environments. This is bad news for you if you're a weekend party girl, because hundreds of brain cells are killed off by weekend drinking binges. To help yourself, either eat your vegetables or take a supplement of vitamins A, C and E.

## 12 Have a fruit salad

Especially after a heavy weekend of partying. Apples will help cleanse your gut, while grapes aid digestion, and pineapple and bananas will restore your blood sugar levels and make you feel less fatigued and more cleansed.

## 13 Indulge in more sex

Sex and orgasms are good for your heart, your self-esteem and your mood. Have sex twice a week and you'll reduce your risk of premature death by 36 per cent and release copious amounts of feel-good endorphins and so also feel good.

## 14 Make yourself laugh

Feeling blue, tired and hungover? Then rent your favourite comedy movie, as research from Johns Hopkins University found that laughing not only ups the production of infection-fighting cells by 25 per cent, but also can lift you out of the doldrums.

## 15 Share the blues with your friends

Your current state may be self-induced but it pays to share, say psychologists, who found that people who had large social groups live longer, stay happier and are less stressed by their bad habits.

## 16 Recharge your mental batteries

Take time out to relax when you're feeling hungover or partied out. Long baths, relaxing music, eye masks, and even comfort food can help restore your psychological and mental energy.

## 17 Sniff yourself better

Certain odours, such as eucalyptus and jasmine, stimulate the part of the brain that makes us alert and active. If you're not into burning candles, choose a shampoo or body wash with one of these ingredients, and lather up.

## 18 Choose green tea

It's a better pick-me-up than coffee because it has over 75 per cent less caffeine, so you'll get a lift without feeling frenetic, plus it will dose you up with antioxidants.

## 19 Prepare in advance for post-party munchies

There's nothing worse than waking up to empty wine bottles and no food. If you know you're going for a wild weekend, make sure your fridge is well stocked in advance with moderate-to-healthy produce, so you don't binge eat on top of your binge drinking.

## 20 Give yourself a break

If you've been partying hard, you need a day to recover. So what if you sit in your PJs, eat cold pizza and guzzle diet cola while you watch soap re-runs? If it makes you feel better, it counts.

# chapter 7

# An A—Z essential party survival guide

Of course, by this stage of the book, you should be adept at putting together a party, looking fabulous at one, surviving potential party problems and getting over the morning after the night before. If you're not, either you've surpassed your lazy tag and skipped five chapters or you are feeling so hungover that this page is swimming before your eyes. Whatever your excuse here's a condensed version of party essentials.

## Abdominals

**Technical version:** the band of muscle that traditionally makes up a flat stomach.

**Lazy girl's version:** the part of your stomach that should not concertina up when you sit down in your party outfit.

### AHAs (alpha hydroxy acids)

**Technical version:** acids found in creams and lotions, which work by speeding up cell renewal and exfoliating the top layer of skin.

**Lazy girl's version:** skin stuff that dissolves the top layer of skin to make your face look smoother and brighter.

### Alcohol

**Technical version:** cocktails, beer, wine – all the things that should be available to your guests.

**Lazy girl's version:** the stuff that can give you a killer hangover.

### Antioxidants

**Technical version:** antioxidants mop up the damage that free radicals, such as pollutants, do to your body. Keep levels high and you'll age slower. Antioxidants can be found in brightly coloured vegetables such as tomatoes, peppers and leafy green vegetables, and also in fruits with a high vitamin C content.

**Lazy girl's version:** the stuff that will stop you looking old.

## Atmosphere

**Technical version:** the feeling people want to experience the second they take off their coats. Best achieved with maximum forethought into lighting, decor, drinks, music and food.

**Lazy girl's version:** does your party 'rock' or not?

## Back pain

**Technical version:** what you'll get from dancing in high heels. Why? Simply because high heels throw your pelvis forward meaning more pressure on your lower back when you walk, never mind when you dance the night away. In women back pain (even if caused by super high heels) is usually because of weak stomach muscles, which means the back muscles have to support both the back and front of the body.

**Lazy girl's version:** best avoided by gaining better posture in your heels by practising walking in them and doing some exercise to firm up your stomach.

### Biceps

**Technical version:** the muscle that should be at the front of the upper arm.

**Lazy girl's version:** the sexy little bump that should miraculously appear when you bend your elbow.

### Body language

**Technical version:** our non-verbal signals that tell people whether we like them, loathe them or adore them.

**Lazy girl's version:** the messages you send out to the people around you without saying a word.

### Calories

**Technical version:** the unit for measuring the energy value of food (so you can work out how much you're taking in, and how much you're burning off).

**Lazy girl's version:** a guaranteed way to tell if you're eating too much (as if you didn't already know).

### Carbohydrates

**Technical version:** foods, such as bread, whole grains, pasta and fruit and vegetables, which are used as a fuel source for the body.

**Lazy girl's version:** food, of which you should aim to eat three portions a day unless you're on the Atkins diet and then you should avoid it at all costs.

## Cocktails

**Technical version:** fancy name for any concoction of spirits, juice, fruits and any soda – best copied from a recipe and not made up on the spot.

**Lazy girl's version:** drinks that look harmless but aren't.

## Conversation

**Technical version:** a key component to any successful party – if you're the host it's your job to keep the conversation going between all the guests who don't know each other.

**Lazy girl's version:** party small talk.

## Costs

**Technical version:** how much this event will cost you. Remember to factor in costs for decoration, food, drink, invitations, cleaning up and, best of all, your outfit.

**Lazy girl's version:** your next-month's credit-card bill.

### Decor

**Technical version:** indoor decoration of the party kind; all the stuff that basically will make your party both memorable and gorgeous to look at.

**Lazy girl's version:** balloons and fairy lights!

### Detox

**Technical version:** a spring-clean system where you limit your diet for a short period of time to very basic food and plain water in order to rid the body of harmful toxins that slow your system down.

**Lazy girl's version:** the diet that eliminates everything you like to eat. Best done by staying in bed for two days.

### Dinner parties

**Technical version:** a sit-down meal, with more than one course, lovingly put together and thought out in advance by you.

**Lazy girl's version:** a meal made by your fair hand for your guests.

## ECP (emergency contraceptive pill)

**Technical version:** previously known as the morning after pill, this pill (which comes in a two-pill form) can actually be taken up to 72 hours after unprotected sex – although the sooner you take it the more effective it is. In some countries the ECP is available over the counter, in others by prescription only.

**Lazy girl's version:** the only post-sex medication that will stop you from getting pregnant.

## Fairy lights

**Technical version:** sexy, sultry and sparkling party tool that can hide most of the decor problems in a venue.

**Lazy girl's version:** the best lazy tool to transform your living room into a party venue.

## Flirting

**Technical version:** another word for body language but this time aimed at attracting someone's attention in a crowded place.

**Lazy girl's version:** how to get him to notice you fancy him!

## Food

**Technical version:** sorry, you have to have some at your party, and crisps and nuts don't count. Food is essential because (a) it stops your guests getting too drunk; (b) it screams good hostess; and (c) it stops your guests going to McDonalds halfway through the night.

**Lazy girl's version:** sustenance to help you and your guests party the whole night through.

## Free radicals

**Technical version:** free radicals are molecules that destroy cells in the body and are found in cigarette smoke, pollution and even air-conditioning units.

**Lazy girl's version:** the hidden stuff that contributes towards ageing.

## Glasses

**Technical version:** whether they be glass, plastic or paper, you'll always need more than you bargained for. Always have two glasses for every guest and you'll be covered.

**Lazy girl's version:** what you'll need plenty of if you don't want guests swigging out of bottles.

## Guests

**Technical version:** the people you want to impress with your amazing hostess abilities, fancy invitations and great party planning. Usually these people will be a combination of friends, work colleagues and friends of friends.

**Lazy girl's version:** the people who bring a bottle or a gift when they arrive at your door.

## GUM (genito-urinary medicine) clinics

**Technical version:** clinics that diagnose and treat people with sexually transmitted infections (STIs), such as HIV, chlamydia and genital bacterial infections. These clinics are found in hospitals and are highly confidential. Records held there do not get sent to your GP or other clinics within the hospital. Find your nearest one by looking in the phone book.

**Lazy girl's version:** sex clinic.

## Hangover

**Technical version:** the by-product of drinking too much, getting dehydrated and ending up with a headache, and other morning-after ailments.

**Lazy girl's version:** alcohol poisoning.

### High heels

**Technical version:** shoes designed to make your legs look longer and sexier when you're doing your stuff on the dance floor.

**Lazy girl's version:** the shoes that will make you wobble when you walk.

### Hostess

**Technical version:** the person throwing the party.

**Lazy girl's version:** the person paying for the drink you're guzzling.

### Invitations

**Technical version:** formal invitations that usually require an RSVP (see below).

**Lazy girl's version:** a way to control how many people arrive at your door on the night of your party.

### Noise

**Technical version:** believe it or not there are strict regulations for this, so warn your neighbours and keep things under control.

**Lazy girl's version:** the stuff you have to keep under control if you want to stop your neighbours pounding on the walls.

## Painkillers

**Technical version:** aspirin, paracetamol and anything that makes you feel better post-party.

**Lazy girl's version:** hangover helpers.

## Planning

**Technical version:** basically the whole of Chapter 1 – read it and weep.

**Lazy girl's version:** all the anxiety and hard work you put into having a party.

## Repetitions

**Technical version:** the number of times you repeat an exercise in one set before moving to a different one.

**Lazy girl's version:** the number of times you have to do an exercise for it to have an effect on your muscles.

## RSVPs

**Technical version:** a request that you make to your guests asking them to let you know whether they're coming or not, usually by a pre-requested date.

**Lazy girl's version:** a way to work out just how much booze and food you need to buy.

## Schmoozing

**Technical version:** working a room to make sure all your guests are having a good time.

**Lazy girl's version:** wandering from person to person and saying something ingratiating.

## Spontaneity

**Technical version:** the instant spark that makes you think it will be a fantastic idea to throw a party right this second.

**Lazy girl's version:** a party without all the planning.

## STIs (sexually transmitted infections)

**Technical version:** nasty diseases such as genital warts, chlamydia and herpes, which are caught when you have unprotected sex: sex without a condom. If you've risked it, hot-foot it along to your nearest GUM clinic to get checked out ASAP.

**Lazy girl's version:** that itch down below.

## Stress

**Technical version:** the name given for pressure added to your life. It may come in the form of emotional problems, and/or work commitments, or be caused by upset plans, someone's behaviour, moving house, getting married or even illness – the list is endless.

**Lazy girl's version:** all those annoying commitments you have to face every day.

## Taxi cabs

**Technical version:** the vehicles that will get rid of all those late-night laggers who just won't go home.

**Lazy girl's version:** the people you'll be calling to help you to get home at 3.00 a.m. Tip: have the number handy, because you won't find it when you're drunk.

## *Themes*

**Technical version:** the factor that determines what kind of party you're going to have and why.

**Lazy girl's version:** a good excuse to have the party 'you' want.

## *Triceps*

**Technical version:** the muscle on the underneath of your upper arm that rarely gets used when lying on the sofa.

**Lazy girl's version:** the batwing part of your arm (your granny has this).

## *Venues*

**Technical version:** the location of your party. It can be your house, a friend's place, a restaurant, a stately home or your local bar – the list is endless if you think creatively.

**Lazy girl's version:** the place where your guests will loiter noisily all night.

## *Vitamins*

**Technical version:** naturally occurring substances, which are essential for a healthy body and life. The best way to get them is through your food intake because this aids their integration into the body and helps them to work effectively.

**Lazy girl's version:** all the nutrients you avoid if you stick to a low-calorie, or junk- and alcohol-based diet.

## Zzzz ... sleep

**Technical version:** sleep is what you'll be gagging for after weeks of partying. Aim for between seven to nine hours a night and you'll be fine.

**Lazy girl's version:** something you'll probably do quite easily after a night out.

# Resources

## UK

### Get-in-shape help

**Dynaband websites**
www.bodysmartUK.com
www.exercise.co.uk/powerbands
www.gb-sports.co.uk
www.sweatybetty.com

**Swiss ball websites**
www.fitball-training.com
www.ukfitnesssupplies.co.uk

**Fitness websites**
www.fitnessheaven.com
www.thefitclub.com
www.thefitmap.com

**Gym equipment websites**
www.personaltrainer.uk.com
www.totallyfitness.com
www.weightlosscenter.co.uk
www.yogamad.com

**Personal trainers**
To find your nearest trainer call National Register of
Personal Trainers
Tel: 020 7407 9223 Website: www.nrpt.co.uk

Association of Personal Trainers
PO Box 6131
London SW9 9XR
Tel: 01424 465333 Website: www.aopt.co.uk

## *Morning-after help*

BPAS (British Pregnancy Advice Service)
Tel: 08457 304030 Website: www.bpas.org

Brook Advisory Centres
Tel: 0800 0185 023 Website: www.brook.org.uk

**Cleaning**
Tips on how to clean up post-party
Website: www.howtocleananything.com

Family Planning Association
FPA contraceptive helpline
Tel: 0845 310 1334 Website: www.fpa.org.uk

Sleep Council
Tel: 0800 018 7923 Website: www.sleepcouncil.org.uk

**Society of Chiropodists & Podiatrists**
The Society of Chiropodists
1 Fellmonger's Path
Tower Bridge Road
London SE1 3LY
Tel: 020 7234 8620 Website: www.feetforlife.org

Stress Management
Tel: 0208 293 4114 Website: www.managingstress.com

Trashed (Website of the National Drugs Helpline)
Tel: 0800 77 66 00 Website: www.trashed.co.uk

### *Party planning, venues and supplies websites*

www.allrecipies.com – good for food ideas
www.partybox.co.uk – party supplies
www.partyproductsdirect.co.uk – good for themed parties
www.perfectvenue.com – database of UK venues
www.majestic.co.uk – good for wine

## *Australia*

www.childrenspartydirectory.com – help for kids' parties
www.fitnessaustralia.com.au – fitness tips
www.fitnessonline.com – personal trainers and gyms
www.onlyfitness.com.au – fitness tips and trainers
www.partypages.com.au – party help
www.sissel-online.com – Swiss ball and gym equipment

## *New Zealand*

www.everybody.co.nz – health and fitness tips
www.gymfit.co.nz – health, nutrition and fitness tips
www.party-oz.com – party planning for NZ and Australia

## *South Africa*

www.bodyline.co.za – nutrition
www.fitnesszone.co.za – gyms, fitness tips, stockists, and
   yoga and Pilates

## *North America*

www.acefitness.org – American Council on Exercise

www.dietiticians.ca – healthy-eating site

www.fitnessusa.com – personal training, gyms and stockists

www.fitter1.com – Swiss ball stockists

www.partyplansplus.com – American party-planning advice

www.performbetter.com – Swiss ball and gym equipment stockists

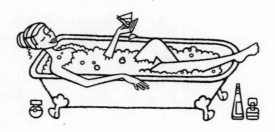

# *index*